Cambridge E

Elements in Publishing
edited b
Samantha Rayner
University College London
Rebecca Lyons
University of Bristol

THE ANGLO-NORMAN
HISTORICAL CANON

Publishing and Manuscript Culture

Jaakko Tahkokallio
University of Helsinki, National Library of Finland

CAMBRIDGE
UNIVERSITY PRESS

CAMBRIDGE
UNIVERSITY PRESS

University Printing House, Cambridge CB2 8BS, United Kingdom

One Liberty Plaza, 20th Floor, New York, NY 10006, USA

477 Williamstown Road, Port Melbourne, VIC 3207, Australia

314–321, 3rd Floor, Plot 3, Splendor Forum, Jasola District Centre, New Delhi – 110025, India

79 Anson Road, #06–04/06, Singapore 079906

Cambridge University Press is part of the University of Cambridge.

It furthers the University's mission by disseminating knowledge in the pursuit of education, learning, and research at the highest international levels of excellence.

www.cambridge.org
Information on this title: www.cambridge.org/9781108713771
DOI: 10.1017/9781108624886

First published 2019

A catalogue record for this publication is available from the British Library.

ISBN 978-1-108-71377-1 Paperback
ISSN 2514-8524 (online)
ISSN 2514-8516 (print)

The Anglo-Norman Historical Canon

Publishing and Manuscript Culture

Elements in Publishing and Book Culture

DOI: 10.1017/9781108624886
First published online: June 2019

Jaakko Tahkokallio
University of Helsinki, National Library of Finland
Author for correspondence: Jaakko Tahkokallio jaakko.tahkokallio@helsinki.fi

ABSTRACT: This Element is a contribution to the ongoing debate on what it meant to publish a book in manuscript. It offers a case study of three twelfth-century Anglo-Norman historians: William of Malmesbury, Henry of Huntingdon, and Geoffrey of Monmouth. It argues that the contemporary success and rapid attainment of canonical authority for their histories were in significant measure the result of successfully conducted publishing activities. These activities are analysed using the concept of a 'publishing circle'. This concept, it is suggested, may have wider utility in the study of authorial publishing in a manuscript culture.

This Element is also available as Open Access on Cambridge Core at doi.org/10.1017/9781108624886

KEYWORDS: historiography, manuscripts, publishing

ISBNs: 9781108713771 (PB), 9781108624886 (OC)
ISSNs: 2514-8524 (online), ISSN 2514-8516 (print)

Contents

1 Introduction   1

2 William of Malmesbury   18

3 Henry of Huntingdon   33

4 Geoffrey of Monmouth   48

5 Conclusions   70

References   78

1 Introduction

Since the emergence of the scholarly field of book history, it has been customary to see the printed book as an agent of change. By being typeset, printed, and issued in large numbers – by being published – texts can penetrate society and change how its members perceive the world. In considering the preprint literary world, our analytical approach has tended towards the opposite direction. We look at the numbers of surviving manuscript copies of a text from the Middle Ages and we typically assess them as signifiers of the interests of the times, as cultural objects and not as evidence of an attempt to distribute a given text. Whereas Aldus Manutius, publishing classical texts in Venice around 1500, is seen as an actor who made a contribution to the diffusion of humanistic modes, the proliferation of copies of Cicero's works in the twelfth century is taken instead to indicate a growing interest in classical Latin literature. The printed book sets change in motion; the manuscript book is merely the effect of change.

Analogically, when we reflect on the literary success of a given work in the world of print, we almost reflexively think about the role publishing played in its making. In a manuscript culture, by way of contrast, the dissemination of a work is typically understood as an organic process, taking place outside the author's control and often extending far beyond his or her lifetime. To a point, this difference in perspective is valid and natural. The printing press makes of publishing a clearly defined action taking place at a specific moment; furthermore, owing to the financial burden involved in printing an edition, it also makes publishing inherently commercial and promotional. In medieval manuscript culture, publishing is not an act similarly defined by any mechanical operation or investment in large-scale production belonging to a particular point in time. As Daniel Hobbins has emphasised, publishing in manuscript culture is always a diffuse process.[1]

We should not, however, assume that this process was typically innocent or void of authorial intentions. What is the point of writing in any context – print, manuscript, or digital – if not for an audience? Printing may have

---

[1]   D. Hobbins, *Authorship and Publicity before Print: Jean Gerson and the Transformation of Late Medieval Learning* (Philadelphia: University of Pennsylvania Press, 2009), p. 154.

raised the stakes by greatly enlarging the potential audience and making a wide distribution much easier to achieve but it did not change the fundamental rationale of publishing as an interface between an author and an audience. What is more, while a limited audience of close associates was enough for some medieval authors, narrative evidence clearly shows that others intended to make their works available in an open literary public sphere, the existence of which seems to have been generally acknowledged. That no single actor could play the distributive role of the printer should not obscure the fact that authorial publishing did happen in the manuscript context and that its fundamental goal was the same as in the age of print: making a new text available to an audience.

In what follows, I present both a methodological suggestion about how authorial publishing can be conceptualised in manuscript culture and an empirical application of this proposed conceptual framework. My key analytical proposition, around which this study is organised, is that authorial publishing in manuscript culture was about creating a task force – a publishing circle – to drive forward the distribution of a text. The publishing circle, again, operated within a wider network of literary connections and modalities of book production which provided the intellectual and material infrastructure for dissemination: in brief, a 'publishing framework'. Methodologically, I suggest that these twin concepts of publishing circle and publishing framework can provide a helpful pair of tools for empirical analysis of authorial publishing in any manuscript context.

The substance of this study consists of an application of this approach to three twelfth-century Anglo-Norman historians. The works which I will examine are the *Historia Anglorum* by Henry of Huntingdon (*c.*1088–1157), *Gesta regum Anglorum* by William of Malmesbury (b. *c.*1090, d. in or after 1142) and *De gestis Britonum* by Geoffrey of Monmouth (d. 1154/5). Besides offering a contribution to the study of publishing in manuscript culture per se, I aim to provide a better vantage point for the appreciation of these works in their historical context. All these texts attained canonical authority soon after their appearance and they came to provide the starting point for all later medieval histories of Britain, whether in Latin or in the vernacular. Indeed, they are still among the most widely read and studied twelfth-century texts from England. My analysis of their publishing histories suggests that this success was not a simple consequence of having written attractive texts but that these authors were actively seeking an audience and literary fame. They were, it seems, also keenly aware that, by so doing, they were participating in a public discourse, one with potentially political implications.

To clarify how my approach differs from previous attempts to conceptualise publishing in a manuscript context, I shall begin by discussing previous work done on this topic. I shall then provide a survey of the wider historical framework of publishing, the key components of which were social networks and the infrastructure of book manufacture. Then, more briefly, it will be necessary to review the nature of the evidence on which this study rests. The reconstruction of the publishing histories themselves, which follows, constitutes the main body of this study, in which the authors are discussed separately. This straightforward narrative structure is necessitated by the complicated nature of the source work involved. While publishing histories are often intricate in the case of print, the disentangling of the messy threads of evidence that allows us to see how publishing took place in manuscript culture is a yet more complicated affair.

1.1 Conceptualising Publishing in Manuscript Culture

Much has been written on medieval authors and authorship and, separately, on readers and readership; but the moment in which a text passed from being an intellectual possession of the author to circulation among potential readers has received little attention until very recently. One important reason for that, as several scholars have noted, is that the words 'publishing' and 'publication' so forcefully conjure images from the world of print as to push aside consideration of what it meant to circulate a book in manuscript.[2] Some commentators, indeed, have gone so far as to question the legitimacy of the concept of 'publishing' in the context of manuscript culture, precisely

[2] See J. Crick and A. Walsham, 'Introduction: Script, Print and History', in J. Crick and A. Walsham (eds.), *The Uses of Script and Print, 1300–1700* (Cambridge: Cambridge University Press, 2004), pp. 1–26, at p. 19; Hobbins, *Authorship and Publicity*, p. 153; and L. Tether, *Publishing the Grail in Medieval and Renaissance France* (Woodbridge: D.S.Brewer, 2017), p. 13.

because its associations with print are so strong.[3] This decision is part of a more general trend which seeks to exercise caution in applying 'post-Gutenbergian' concepts to medieval literature, placing its emphasis on the malleability of medieval texts and their otherness from the world of print, in which text is 'set'. Such scepticism, however, has its limits and an accumulating body of scholarship is now making a well-argued case for the usefulness of the concept of publishing in manuscript culture, not least for what it can contribute to an understanding of authors and contemporary audiences.[4] There can be no doubt, as Daniel Hobbins has observed, that 'the very notion of publishing is premodern'.[5]

While the study of publishing in manuscript has been emerging as a scholarly field, its subject has proved resistant to definition. This has much to do with the Gutenbergian undertones of how we conceive of the process. In a print culture, publishing is neatly defined by the sudden multiplication

[3] S. G. Nichols, 'Introduction: Philology in a Manuscript Culture', *Speculum*, 65 (1990), 1–10, at 6; E. L. Eisenstein, *The Printing Press as an Agent of Change: Communications and Cultural Transformations in Early Modern Europe*, vol. 1 (Cambridge: Cambridge University Press, 1979), p. 11.

[4] J. C. Laidlaw, 'Christine de Pizan – a Publisher's Progress', *Modern Language Review*, 82 (1987), 35–75; A. I. Doyle, 'Publication by Members of the Religious Orders', in J. Griffiths and D. Pearsall (eds.), *Book Production and Publishing in Britain 1375–1475* (Cambridge: Cambridge University Press, 1989), pp. 109–23; L. Earp, 'Machaut's Role in the Production of Manuscripts of His Works', *Journal of the American Musicological Society*, 42 (1989), 461–503; F. Riddy, '"Publication" before Print: The Case of Julian of Norwhich', in J. Crick and A. Walsham (eds.), *The Uses of Script and Print, 1300–1700* (Cambridge: Cambridge University Press, 2004), pp. 29–49; Hobbins, Authorship and Publicity; R. Sharpe, 'Anselm as Author: Publishing in the Late Eleventh Century', *The Journal of Medieval Latin*, 19 (2009), 1–87; L. Tether, 'Revisiting the Manuscripts of *Perceval* and the Continuations: Publishing Practices and Authorial Transition', *Journal of the International Arthurian Society*, 2 (2014), 20–45; A. N. J. Dunning, 'Alexander Neckam's Manuscripts and the Augustinian Canons of Oxford and Cirencester', unpublished PhD thesis, University of Toronto (2016); and Tether, *Publishing the Grail*.

[5] Hobbins, *Authorship and Publicity*, p. 153.

of copies of a text by the printing press and their ensuing dissemination. This typically commercially driven technical operation both turns a text into a public intellectual commodity, outside of the author's direct control, and makes it generally available as a material object. These two sides of the publishing action – the immaterial and the material – are implicit in our post-Gutenbergian understanding of publishing. While I would argue that both release and dissemination were objectives of medieval authors and editors as well, the two actions are not, in the context of manuscript publication, similarly brought together by any technological matrix.

The fact that these two fundamental elements of publishing cannot be encapsulated into a single moment has catalysed attempts to define publishing in a manuscript context by concentrating on one or the other. On the immaterial side, it has been proposed, most concisely by Paul Meyvaert, that publishing should be equated with the author's act of giving a copy of his work to someone else, accompanied by their permission to make copies of it.[6] This is a conceptually neat and economical definition of the release-of-intellectual-property aspect of publishing. It is publishing in this sense which many works of medieval literary history and prefaces to editions of medieval texts typically discuss, and certainly this was an aspect of publishing of which medieval authors themselves were conscious.[7] However, semantically justified as it is, this definition severs the act of release from any necessary connection to the actual promotion and dissemination that the work consequently had. As an analytical conceptual tool, it also fails to open new perspectives. Pinpointing publishing at the single moment of release does not really help us to understand how publishing functioned as an interface between an author and his or her audience; and yet understanding that very relationship is one of the main reasons for the study of the phenomenon in the first place.

---

[6] P. Meyvaert, 'Medieval Notions of Publication: The "Unpublished" Opus Caroli regis contra synodum and the Council of Frankfort (794)', *The Journal of Medieval Latin*, 12 (2002), 78–89, at 81 and passim. See also Hobbins, *Authorship and Publicity*, pp. 153–4.

[7] See, in particular, Meyvaert, 'Medieval Notions of Publication', and Sharpe, 'Anselm as Author', 1–2.

Aware of such problems, other scholars have defined publishing in a manuscript context by focussing entirely on aspects of material distribution, disregarded by the release-centred interpretation. A distribution-centred definition has been most explicitly argued for by Leah Tether in her seminal work on the role of the makers of books in the promotion and distribution of the Grail romances.[8] Other scholars, too, have interpreted the late medieval urban book craftsman as the closest possible medieval equivalent to the modern publisher.[9] This is a perfectly valid angle of analysis and, indeed, such craftsmen were making a living by selling reproductions of texts, the analogue of what printers would later do. Furthermore, such an emphasis is valuable in softening the contrast between medieval and modern book cultures, still too starkly perceived outside the specialist domains of book history. Nevertheless, this distribution-centred definition is not equally helpful in analysing the case of an author (and/or editor) launching a specific work with the intention of making it widely available, i.e. the case of authorial publishing.[10]

This brings us, finally, to what I would characterise as the third, process-centred approach into conceptualising publishing in manuscript culture. To bridge the disjuncture between release and dissemination, other scholars have sought to define the ways in which the interface functioned between author and distribution. In a rare early contribution on the topic, published in 1913, R. K. Root proposed four different categories of preprint publication, which entail both release and distribution, or at least promotion: publication by presenting a text to a patron, publication by public reading, publication sanctioned by a religious authority, and commercial publication by making the text available to urban professional scribes.[11] These and similar models for the preprint author–distribution interface have been

[8] Tether, *Publishing the Grail*.

[9] H. S. Bennett, 'The Production and Dissemination of Vernacular Manuscripts in the Fifteenth Century', *The Library*, Fifth Series, 1 (1946), 167–78; Riddy, '"Publication" before Print', 30, 36.

[10] For late medieval authors conscious of their roles as publishers, see Laidlaw, 'Christine de Pizan', Earp, 'Machaut's Role', and Hobbins, *Authorship and Publicity*.

[11] R. K. Root, 'Publication before Printing', *PMLA*, 28 (1913), 417–31.

discussed by other scholars, with patronage and 'official', ecclesiastically approved publication typically receiving most attention.[12] Also, the possibility of a manner of publishing by non-publishing, i.e. by simply slipping a text into 'organic' circulation, has been noted.[13]

All the phenomena classified by the concepts above (except probably strictly commercial publishing) did indeed happen.[14] However, as has been implicitly recognised in the aforementioned studies and made explicit in Felicity Riddy's overview of Root's ideas, these, or indeed any, rigid categories do not adequately cover how texts were in fact made available to readers in a manuscript culture.[15] It must be kept in mind that these categories are categories of analysis – scholarly abstractions rather than contemporary conceptualisations reflecting established medieval practices – and their value depends on whether they help us to understand how real publishing happened in manuscript culture. In an empirical enquiry, they

---

[12] K. J. Holzknecht, 'Literary Patronage in the Middle Ages', unpublished PhD dissertation, University of Pennsylvania (1923); Bennett, 'Production and Dissemination'; Doyle, 'Publication by Members of the Religious Orders', and Dunning, 'Alexander Neckam's Manuscripts'.

[13] Bennett, 'Production and Dissemination', 170.

[14] The idea of commercial scrivener publication depended to some extent on the so-called bookshop theory, i.e. the assumption, since discredited, that there would have been scriptorium-like workshops in late medieval cities, in which teams of scribes could have produced multiple copies of a text. The contours of the debate can be followed in L. H. Loomis, 'The Auchinleck Manuscript and a Possible London Bookshop of 1330–1340', *PMLA*, 57 (1942), 595–627; G. Dempster, 'Manly's Conception of the Early History of the Canterbury Tales', *PMLA*, 61 (1946), 379–415; T. A. Shonk, 'A Study of the Auchinleck Manuscript: Bookmen and Bookmaking in the Early Fourteenth Century', *Speculum*, 60 (1985), 71–91; C. P. Christianson, 'The Rise of London's Book-Trade', in L. Hellinga and J. B. Trapp (eds.), *The Cambridge History of the Book in Britain*, vol. 3 (Cambridge: Cambridge University Press, 1999), pp. 128–47, at p. 130, and M. B. Parkes, *Their Hands Before Our Eyes: A Closer Look at Scribes. The Lyell Lectures Delivered in the University of Oxford 1999* (Aldershot: Ashgate, 2008), pp. 51–3.

[15] Riddy, '"Publication" before Print', pp. 30–7.

can appear potentially misleading, for it is obvious that the actual publishing of a text did not need to happen according to the model the case might appear to follow: the named dedicatee was not necessarily the key person in the promotion of a text apparently published under patronage; the force which drove to literary success a specific text published 'officially' within a religious order may have been the influence of an individual abbot or bishop, or that of a particular personal network to which the author had access; a text published by a secular clerk may have been adopted for distribution within a religious order. Needless to say, a single author (or editor) may have relied on several different mechanisms for disseminating his or her work.

This is not to say that these ways of putting texts into circulation did not exist and we shall frequently encounter the phenomena they refer to – patronage in particular – in this study. However, the nature of the present undertaking necessitates a different kind of functionally defined analytical tool. Over the following pages, I shall be studying three authors who, I argue, were actively trying to publish their works, in the modern sense of making them available to various audiences. They were concerned both to release intellectual content and to seek ways to have it materially distributed. My goal is to reconstruct empirically as much of these processes as possible, rather than seeking instances of this or that predefined method of publishing. The key concept of this study, by which I define the scope of this author-driven publishing activity, is that of a 'publishing circle'. By a publishing circle, I mean those individuals and institutions which were actively engaged in the authorial effort to spread the text. This certainly includes, in this case, many of the dedicatees but it is not limited to them, for, as we shall see, there is strong evidence that other agents were also involved in the publishing process, while the role of the apparent patron could remain very limited.

The concept of the publishing circle is also an attempt to answer a perennial question asked of publishing in a manuscript context: at what point does publishing turn into dissemination? My solution approaches this problem from a functionalist point of view. I make the assumption that the essential constituents of book publishing are the release of intellectual content on the one hand and material distribution on the other, and that publishing is implicitly promotional. Thus, a publishing circle ends where the (in this case authorial) intention to advance the circulation of the work fades away. The circle, in other words, is a publishing task force which, in a loose sense, is recruited by the author. The focus of study for this Element falls on three particular publishing circles but, before introducing them, we need briefly to look at the framework in which all these circles took shape.

1.2 The Publishing Framework: Audiences of History and the Modalities of Book Production in Post-Conquest England and the Anglo-Norman Realm

During the reigns of Henry I and Stephen, several narrative histories were produced which came to define the perception of Britain's past for centuries to come.[16] The three authors of this study – Henry of Huntingdon, William of Malmesbury, and Geoffrey of Monmouth – were the central actors in this undertaking. While they were not the only ones writing on historical topics at the time, it was their work that came to dominate the historiographical canon in Britain. Both their extensive influence on contemporary and near-contemporary historiography and their own popularity, as indicated by the number of surviving manuscript copies of their works, have been abundantly documented.[17] Thinking of the three as a group is, furthermore, not

---

[16] As James Campbell put it, '[t]he greatest advances in the study and understanding of Anglo-Saxon history made before the nineteenth century were those of the twelfth'; J. Campbell, 'Some Twelfth-Century Views of the Anglo-Saxon Past', in J. Campbell, *Essays in Anglo-Saxon History* (London: The Hambledon Press, 1986), pp. 209–228, at p. 209.

[17] On the influence, for Henry, see A. Gransden, *Historical Writing in England: c. 550 to c. 1307* (Ithaca, NY: Cornell University Press, 1974), pp. 212, 226, 260 (n. 97), 261, 264, 363, 412, 434, 444; for William, *ibid.*, pp. 144 (n. 57), 434, 444, and W. Stubbs, 'Preface', in *Willelmi Malmesbiriensis monachi de Gestis regum Anglorum libri quinque*, Rolls Series, 90, ed. W. Stubbs (London: Her Majesty's Stationery Office by Eyre and Spottiswoode, 1887), pp. ix–cxlvii, at pp. xcii–xciii; and, for Geoffrey, L. Keeler, *Geoffrey of Monmouth and the Late Latin Chroniclers 1300–1500* (Berkeley:University of California, 1946); R. H. Fletcher, *The Arthurian Material in the Chronicles, Especially Those of Great Britain and France* (Cambridge, MA:

simply a later classification. Geoffrey commented explicitly on the works of Henry and William, in a manner which shows that he understood them to be members of a group participating in the same debate,[18] and the texts themselves demonstrate that Geoffrey and Henry at least had access to each other's work.[19] What is more, they shared a network of patronage. Both Geoffrey and Henry dedicated works to Alexander, bishop of Lincoln, while both Geoffrey and William offered dedications to Robert, earl of

Harvard University Press, 1906), and J. Tahkokallio, 'French Chroniclers and the Credibility of Geoffrey of Monmouth's History of the Kings of Britain, c. 1150–1225', in H. Tétrel and G. Veysseyre (eds.), *L'Historia regum Britannie et Les 'Bruts en Europe': Traductions, adaptations, réappropriations (XIIᵉ–XVIᵉ Siècle)* (Paris: Classiques Garnier, 2015), pp. 53–67. The numbers of surviving manuscripts: Henry of Huntingdon, *Historia Anglorum*, 45 medieval copies (13 from the twelfth century), William of Malmesbury, *Gesta regum Anglorum*, 36 medieval copies (19 from the twelfth century), Geoffrey of Monmouth, *De gestis Britonum*, 225 medieval copies (c.70 from the twelfth century). For the manuscripts, see D. Greenway, 'Introduction', in Henry of Huntingdon, *Historia Anglorum*, ed. and trans. D. Greenway (Oxford: Clarendon Press, 1996), pp. xxiii–clxxii; R. M. Thomson and M. Winterbottom, 'Introduction', in William of Malmesbury, *Gesta Regum Anglorum: The History of the English Kings*, vol. 1, ed. R. Thomson and M. Winterbottom (Oxford: Clarendon Press, 1998), pp. xiii–xxxii; J. Crick, *Historia Regum Britannie of Geoffrey of Monmouth III: A Summary Catalogue of the Manuscripts* (Cambridge: D.S.Brewer, 1989), and J. Tahkokallio, 'Update to the List of Manuscripts of Geoffrey of Monmouth's *Historia Regum Britanniae*', *Arthurian Literature*, 32 (2015), 187–203.

[18] Geoffrey of Monmouth, *The History of the Kings of Britain. An Edition and Translation of De Gestis Britonum*, ed. M. Reeve, trans. N. Wright (Woodbridge: Boydell Press, 2007), §208 (p. 281).

[19] For Henry's encounter with Geoffrey's work, see N. Wright, 'The Place of Henry of Huntingdon's *Epistola Ad teksti Warinum* in the Text-History of Geoffrey of Monmouth's *Historia Regum Britannie*: A Preliminary Investigation', in G. Jondorf and D. N. Dumville (eds.), *France and the British Isles in the Middle Ages and Renaissance: Essays by Members of Girton College, Cambridge, in Memory of Ruth Morgan* (Woodbridge: Boydell Press, 1991), pp. 71–113. For Henry's influence on Geoffrey, see J. S. P. Tatlock, *The Legendary History of Britain* (Berkeley: University of California Press, 1950), pp. 34, 67, 121, 281.

Gloucester.[20] Indeed, while there were also other patrons involved, addressed by just one of the writers, these two were clearly the most important ones (Alexander for Henry, Robert for Geoffrey and William).

All of the dedicatees involved in our cases – bishops, counts, kings, and an empress – were leading members of the Anglo-Norman aristocracy and this elite provided one social network that these authors utilised in promoting their works. Identity makes history relevant and twelfth-century England was no exception. This particular burst of historical writing has been interpreted, no doubt correctly, as ultimately reflecting the reconfiguring of elite identity following the rupture of the Norman Conquest.[21] The fact that history was written in Latin did not mean that its intended audience was exclusively, or even primarily, ecclesiastical. As the vernacular languages were not yet (or not any more, in the case of Old English) available as literary vehicles, many secular aristocrats of the era received education in Latin, often beyond its rudiments.[22] Even more importantly, the bureaucratic expansion of the period meant that men who had clerical education but were not necessarily pursuing an ecclesiastical career, at least in a traditional sense, were present in lay courts in increasing numbers.[23] In

---

[20] These dedications will be given detailed discussion in what follows.

[21] See R. W. Southern, 'Presidential Address: Aspects of the European Tradition of Historical Writing: 4. The Sense of the Past', *Transactions of the Royal Historical Society*, 23 (1973), 243–63; L. Ashe, *Fiction and History in England, 1066–1200* (Cambridge: Cambridge University Press, 2008), pp. 1–9, and, from a different perspective, E. A. Winkler, *Royal Responsibility in Anglo-Norman Historical Writing* (Oxford: Oxford University Press, 2017), pp. 3–13. For the questions of identity, see, in particular, J. Gillingham, 'Henry of Huntingdon and the Twelfth-Century Revival of the English Nation', in J. Gillingham, *English in the Twelfth Century* (Woodbridge: Boydell Press, 2000), pp. 123–44.

[22] M. T. Clanchy, *From Memory to Written Record: England 1066–1307*, 2nd ed. (Oxford: Blackwell, 1993), pp. 224–52 and M. Aurell, *Le chevalier lettré: Savoir et conduite de l'aristocratie aux XIIe et XIIIe siècles* ([Paris]: Fayard, 2011).

[23] For instance, in France, Henry the Liberal, first count of Champagne, created sixty new canonicates for the chapel of Saint-Étienne (opened in 1157) alone, the main task of these clerics being to provide the bureaucratic expertise for the running of the county; see T. Evergates, *The Aristocracy in the County of*

the context of the Anglo-Norman realm of the second quarter of the twelfth century, it is reasonable to assume that Latin works of secular history communicated, and were meant to communicate, in this unified aristocratic sphere, defined more by family descent and access to political power than by any division into lay and ecclesiastical domains.

Besides this aristocratic network, and partly overlapping it, there existed the networks of religious orders. The effects of the eleventh-century Benedictine reform of Normandy and its post-Conquest English sequel were still being felt in the second quarter of the twelfth century. This period also witnessed a proliferation of houses of regular canons and, in England as elsewhere, the high point of the expansion of the more recently launched Cistercian monastic order.[24] These initiatives manifested themselves in active book production and the promotion of scholarship, historical writing included. Monasteries were the most history-conscious corporations of the twelfth century and it is inevitable that their inmates would always populate the audience for any historical work. For a monastic institution, the identity-building significance of history was based on an ecclesiastical view of the past, but the monks themselves, who came principally from the aristocratic stratum, also shared the same broad national and political concerns of their secular peers.

At the same time, neither the monastic nor the aristocratic interest in history was governed solely by the concerns of identity. Indeed, our well-justified view that history is, ultimately, about identity is really no more than that – a well-justified view and not something on which there was ever much explicit contemporary comment. In both contexts, history was

Champagne, 1100–1300 (Philadelphia: University of Pennsylvania Press, 2007), p. 16.

[24] For an up-to-date discussion on the monastic expansion (concerning only Yorkshire but setting the outline for the whole of England), see J. E. Burton, *The Monastic Order in Yorkshire, 1069–1215* (Cambridge: Cambridge University Press, 1999). D. Knowles, *The Monastic Order in England: A History of Its Development from the Times of St Dunstan to the Fourth Lateran Council 940–1216*, 2nd ed. (Cambridge: Cambridge University Press, 1963), pp. 83–190, remains a helpful overview.

consumed for reasons which can be described as scholarly and literary, and such interests are more often visible in twelfth-century reflections on history's purpose. Texts about the past could be read and listened to for the sake of scholarly learnedness, for moral edification, to learn Latin, for simple entertainment, or indeed any combination of these (and no doubt other) reasons.[25] Such interests, again, were in no way a prerogative of the English or Anglo-Normans. Around these broadly speaking scholarly approaches to history we can define a further, third network of dissemination. In the course of the late eleventh century, cathedral-school education in the Rhineland, Flanders, and the northern half of France entered a phase of significant expansion.[26] Simultaneously, such education turned into a completely international affair, the French schools of the early twelfth century in particular attracting scholars from an ever-widening territory.[27] This scholarly network intersected with the aristocratic and monastic worlds as men with a school background became courtiers, bishops, monks, and abbots. While the works examined in this present study address the history of a specific geographical area, their circulation depended also on these international academic networks, a kind of a twelfth-century *res publica litterarum*.

These were the three principal social networks that the distribution of historical works, in the second quarter of the twelfth century, could hope to utilise. What determined how precisely the dissemination of texts took place within (and between) these networks was the available modalities of book production. These constitute the other main component of the publishing

[25] M. Kempshall, *Rhetoric and the Writing of History, 400–1500* (Manchester: Manchester University Press, 2011) provides a good overview of broadly scholarly interests in history in the Middle Ages.

[26] For an overview of this development, see C. S. Jaeger, *The Envy of Angels: Cathedral Schools and Social Ideals in Medieval Europe, 950–1200* (Philadelphia: University of Pennsylvania Press, 1994); P. Delhaye, 'L'Organisation scolaire au XIIe siècle', *Traditio*, 5 (1947), 211–68, and G. Paré, A. Brunet, and P. Tremblay, *La Renaissance du XIIe siècle: les écoles et l'enseignement* (Paris: J. Vrin, 1933).

[27] For a close analysis of the 'international' students at Laon school, see C. Giraud, *Per verba magistri: Anselme de Laon et son école au XIIe siècle* (Turnhout: Brepols, 2010), pp. 115–49.

framework and need to be briefly examined. The first observation is a caveat. That is, the rigidity or culturally fixed nature of such modalities should not be overplayed, for manuscript book production was always a decentralised affair and the minimal level of technical infrastructure was low. All that was (and is) needed was an exemplar, a person who could write, and the necessary writing materials. Those being the conditions, highly idiosyncratic books, produced in highly idiosyncratic circumstances, could, and occasionally did, materialise. Nevertheless, like all craft activities, book production was also dependent on technical skills and cultural information, which tended to be concentrated in the hands of fully professional or (more often) semi-professional specialists.

In the early Middle Ages, such concentrations of capabilities tended to be found in religious communities and, in the twelfth century, such communities were still a crucial feature in the landscape of book production. Most importantly, they remained the principal repositories of texts, offering long-term preservation while also functioning as textual supply centres, a role in which we shall encounter them at a later point in this discussion. However, religious communities no longer dominated the actual making of books. While men and women in religious orders certainly continued to copy books, occasionally producing even large numbers of them, it has become increasingly clear over the last few decades that a growing share of the monastic demand for texts was now being supplied by paid scribal labour.[28]

The early medieval subsistence economy, in which monasteries persisted as self-sufficient textual citadels, was being turned into a market-based one

---

[28] No up-to-date synthesis of this development exists, but see, e.g., C. Nordenfalk, *Codex Caesareus Upsaliensis* (Stockholm: Almqvist & Wiksell, 1971), pp. 136–7, 147–8; K. Berg, *Studies in Tuscan Twelfth-Century Illumination* (Oslo: Universitetsforlaget, 1968), pp. 205–2; F. Avril, 'A quand remontent les premiers ateliers d'enlumineurs laïcs à Paris', *Les Dossiers de l'archéologie*, 16 (1976), 36–44; P. Stirnemann, 'Où ont été fabriqués les livres de la glose ordinaire dans la première moitié du XIIe siècle?', in F. Gasparri (ed.), *Le XIIe siècle: Mutations et renouveau en France dans la première moitié du XIIe siècle* (Paris: Cahiers du Léopard d'Or, 1994), pp. 257–301, and M. Gullick, 'Professional Scribes in Eleventh- and Twelfth-Century England', *English Manuscript Studies, 1100–1700*, 7 (1998), 1–24.

with regard to books. The emergence of a rudimentary market for the labour of book craftsmen was radically reshaping the publishing framework in the period treated by this study and the monasteries were but one client on the demand side of this equation. The incipient commercialisation of production coincided with the rise of the cathedral schools and it seems highly likely, although as yet largely unproven, that the schools brought about the increase in both demand for scribal labour (scholars needed books) and its supply (scholars, students in particular, were frequently short of money and could copy books for reward). We do know, after all, that the slightly later emergence of book manufacture as a properly organised urban craft, along the lines of other such crafts, around the turn of the twelfth century, took place in dialogue with the emergence of properly institutionalised independent establishments of higher education such as the universities.[29]

While commercialisation is a useful long-term framework for thinking about this process, it should be underlined that these changes did not mean that most books, in the second quarter of the twelfth century, would have been produced on commission in a monetised commercial market as we might understand it. A large share of the scribal workforce was affiliated to a particular royal, noble, or ecclesiastical household and we must assume that, for example, episcopal or comital chancery scribes and their apprentices or other literate helpers were put to work copying books as well.[30] In this respect, there were clear continuities with the earlier modes of monastic book production, for, in both cases, the making of a book would be a project

---

[29] The classic study is R. Rouse and M. Rouse, *Manuscripts and Their Makers: Commercial Book Producers in Medieval Paris, 1200–1500*, 2 vols. (Turnhout: Brepols, 2000).

[30] An early example is provided by the scribes working for Bishop Leofric of Exeter (d. 1072). See T. A. M. Bishop, 'Notes on Cambridge Manuscripts', *Transactions of the Cambridge Bibliographical Society*, 2 (1954–8), 185–99. As was observed by Bishop (*ibid.*, 197), scribes could also (and perhaps more often did) depend on the person rather than the office, following the same individual through the various steps of his career as a member of his *familia*. I owe this reference to the kindness of James Willoughby.

taking place within a household. Collaboration between household members (whether monastic or secular) and truly professional itinerant book craftsmen was likewise always possible and complicates this picture further. On the whole, however, the new dynamism of the distribution framework, enabled by the growth of the scribal workforce, was redefining twelfth-century literary culture and the culture of the book. The social networks of dissemination – also monastic ones – became increasingly reliant on these mechanisms and this interaction was changing the overall framework for the publishing of Latin texts. It was becoming more responsive and better suited to making texts available to readers – better suited to authorial publishing.

From the viewpoint of a later perspective, I would argue that the publishing framework was already taking the shape it would have in the later Middle Ages, in which urban book production catered for an international, scholarly readership as its core clientele. While the scholarship on medieval publishing has concentrated on the vernacular late Middle Ages,[31] it was Latin that dominated literary production and, until the end of the Middle Ages, set the standard for book culture.[32] It was the making of Latin books that catalysed the professionalisation and commercialisation of bookmaking and also led to new inventions in book design and production, such as gloss layouts, indexes, and production by pecia. There are two

---

[31] Root, 'Publication before Printing'; Bennett, 'Production and Dissemination'; Laidlaw, 'Christine de Pizan'; P. J. Lucas, *From Author to Audience: John Capgrave and Medieval Publication* (Dublin: University College Dublin Press, 1997); Riddy, '"Publication" before Print', and Tether, 'Revisiting the Manuscripts of *Perceval*'.

[32] It is certain that Latin books were produced in by far the greatest numbers until the early modern period. Even in the incunable period, in which new markets were discovered for vernacular works and translations, 70 per cent of printed editions were of Latin texts. This has been calculated from the *Incunabula Short Title Catalogue*, which, at the time of writing, lists 30,527 editions, of which 21,328 are in Latin. J. Trevitt, *Five Hundred Years of Printing by S. H. Steinberg*, rev. ed. (London: British Library and Oak Knoll Press, 1996), p. 54 mentions that three-quarters of incunabular copies (as opposed to editions) were in Latin but does not document how this result was calculated.

particularly thorough case studies of Latin publishing in manuscript – Richard Sharpe's seminal article on Anselm of Canterbury and Daniel Hobbins's monograph on Jean Gerson.[33] This present case study aims to provide a view on the state of affairs one chronological step forward from the world of Anselm, a monk and an archbishop, towards the late medieval international scholarly world of Gerson, a university man.

1.3 A Note on the Sources

The empirical content of this book – the reconstruction of the publishing histories of the three Anglo-Norman historians – is built on three bodies of evidence. The first, and obvious, group of sources is formed of the dedicatory prefaces and letters and authorial references to the matter of publishing. The second is formed of the textual histories. It should be acknowledged at the outset that this Element is deeply indebted to the editors of the studied works and one hopes that the use to which this evidence is put successfully advocates the value of such careful textual scholarship, not only as a means of achieving a reliable source text but also as an indispensable source in the study of medieval book culture. The last source of evidence is constituted by the early manuscripts, most of which have been studied first-hand.

As evidence, textual history and the witness of manuscripts differ in their natures from narrative sources and documents. Their testimony is almost never quite as unambiguous. Rather, they align with archaeological sources, in the sense that we can only draw historical conclusions from this evidence after a layer of interpretation has been imposed on it concerning such fundamental questions as date, origin, and the context of making. Even then, such interpretations tend to give us probabilities rather than certainties. However, this kind of weak or indirect evidence, while it has its deficiencies, is the only kind of evidence we have for historical phenomena which contemporaries did not document or describe, such as publishing. The congruence of weak evidence allows us in this case to reconstruct, with sufficient probability, phenomena which we would not otherwise, with certainty, see at all.

---

[33] Sharpe, 'Anselm as Author', 6.

2 William of Malmesbury

William of Malmesbury was one of the most learned Latin scholars of his day. We know very little about his early life but he was born not far away from the Benedictine abbey of Malmesbury (Wilts), which he entered at an early age and from where he may have been sent to Glastonbury, Canterbury, or both, for further education.[34] William's literary output was prolific, consisting of history, hagiography, *florilegia*, and biblical exegesis.[35] This study will concentrate on the publishing history of his most successful work, the *Gesta regum Anglorum* (*GRA*), but it will also examine more briefly those of his other historical compositions – the *Gesta pontificum Anglorum* (*GPA*) and the *Historia novella* (HN) – to help us better understand William as a publisher.

The genesis of the *GRA* went back to William's encounter with Matilda (d. 1118), queen of King Henry I. According to William, she had first asked William for an account of the family history of St Aldhelm, founder of Malmesbury and her own relative. Once this had been composed, Matilda requested that William proceed with a more comprehensive history of the English.[36] The substance of this project, which became the *GRA*, was finished *c*.1125, and chronologically William never continued this narrative any further, even though he lived until (at least) 1142.

Very soon after the end of his history, in 1125, a fair copy (T) was produced from William's draft (W1) and, from this copy, descended the

---

[34] R. M. Thomson, *William of Malmesbury*, rev. ed. (Woodbridge: Boydell Press, 2003), pp. 4–5.

[35] For William, see D. H. Farmer, 'William of Malmesbury's Life and Works', *The Journal of Ecclesiastical History*, 13 (1962), 39–54 and R. Thomson, 'Malmesbury, William of (b. c. 1090, d. in or after 1142), Historian, Man of Letters, and Benedictine Monk', *Oxford Dictionary of National Biography*, http://www.oxforddnb.com/view/10.1093/ref:odnb/9780198614128.001.0001/odnb-9780198614128-e-29461, accessed 4 April 2018.

[36] William of Malmesbury, *Gesta regum Anglorum: The History of the English Kings*, ed. R. M. Thomson and M. Winterbottom, 2 vols. (Oxford: Clarendon Press, 1998–9), vol. 1, Ep.ii.4–5 (pp. 8–9).

earliest textual family of the *GRA*, the so-called T version.[37] The manuscript of T itself (which does not survive) did not receive any integral dedication but two letters were written to accompany it and they, together with the manuscript evidence, allow us to see how the first steps in the publishing of the work were taken.[38] These letters, both of which accompanied T, announced the work to King David of Scotland and Matilda, Henry I's daughter, usually called Empress Matilda because of her previous marriage to Henry V of Germany and to differentiate her from her mother, Queen Matilda (d. 1118), King David's sister and the original commissioner of the *GRA*.

This curious set of letters allows us to fix the presentation of the T manuscript and the beginning of the circulation of the *GRA* to a specific historical moment. The letter addressing David asked him to accept and authorise the *GRA* and to take care that both the book and the messenger from Malmesbury accompanying it be conducted to the empress.[39] One may wonder whether this authorisation and such help in delivery were really needed and, indeed, David was not addressed simply so that he could add his stamp of authority. Malmesbury Abbey had been without an abbot since 1118 and the second half of the letter begged David to remedy this situation.[40]

---

[37] Thomson and Winterbottom, 'Introduction' (*GRA*, vol. 1), p. xv and pp. xxii–xxiii. I am following Thomson and Winterbottom's assumption that T was the presentation copy (*ibid.*, p. xv) but it is of course possible that there existed an intermediary copy between William's draft and T. Since it does not affect my argumentation whether or not this was the case, there is no reason to bring this complication to the text.

[38] The letters were first reported and published in E. Könsgen, 'Zwei Unbekannte Briefe zu den Gesta regum Anglorum des Wilhelm von Malmesbury', *Deutsches Archiv für Erforschung des Mittelalters*, 31 (1975), 204–14.

[39] 'Hinc est quod Anglorum Regum Gesta uestra regia auctoritate dominae nostrae imperatrici nepti uestrae destinare non timuimus ... Suspiciat ergo excellentia uestra, regum optime, a pauperculo et desolato cetu uestro hereditarium munus, et dominae imperatrici una cum nostro legato uestra etiam auctoritate deferri curate'; William of Malmesbury, *GRA* Ep.i.2–3 (pp. 3–4).

[40] See M. Chibnall, *The Empress Matilda: Queen Consort, Queen Mother, and Lady of the English* (Oxford: Blackwell, 1991), pp. 46–7.

A Scottish king had no prerogative to appoint abbots to a Wiltshire monastery, however, and the monks must have hoped that he would exercise his influence in the English court, where he had spent a lengthy period (from Michaelmas 1126 until summer of 1127) just after the *GRA* had been finished.[41] This hypothesis is compatible with what is known about the movements of Henry I's court. The first documentary trace of Henry's arrival in September 1126 is a charter issued at Portsmouth. This is followed by a series of charters given at Rockingham, in the East Midlands.[42] King David does not appear as a witness in any of these, even though one of the Rockingham charters (*Regesta*, no. 1459), confirming Walter Espec's gifts to Kirkham Priory, has a long witness list with all the important names of the court present. However, we find King David at the head of the witness list in a charter issued at Woodstock, around fifty miles from Malmesbury and evidently familiar to William himself, sometime in the autumn of 1126.[43] The likely conclusion is that David was met by the monks of Malmesbury in 1126 as he was making his way towards the meeting of the court and that a representative from Malmesbury joined his entourage with the book.

In the context of this particularly momentous assize of the royal court, the petition for assistance towards an introduction to Matilda does not seem in the least absurd. It was David's sister (and Empress Matilda's mother) who had commissioned the *GRA*; and David himself, having spent his youth in Henry I's court, was a relatively familiar figure to the Malmesbury monks. This was not the case with Empress Matilda. She had been in

[41] On David's itinerary, see R. Oram, *David I: The King Who Made Scotland* (Stroud: Tempus, 2004), pp. 79–82.

[42] See C. W. Hollister, *Henry I* (New Haven, CT: Yale University Press, 2001), p. 316 and C. Johnson and H. A. Cronne (eds.), *Regesta Regum Anglo-Normannorum, 1066–1154, vol. 2, Regesta Henrici Primi 1100–1135* (Oxford: Clarendon Press, 1956), no. 1448 (Portsmouth) and nos. 1458–63 (Rockingham).

[43] Johnson and Cronne (eds.), *Regesta Regum Anglo-Normannorum 1066–1154*, vol. 2, no. 1466 and nos. 1464–70 were all issued at Woodstock. Woodstock was a royal hunting ground and it also contained Henry I's menagerie of wild animals, which we know about only thanks to William's report in the *GRA*, apparently based on first-hand observation. William of Malmesbury, *GRA* v.410 (pp. 740–1).

Germany since 1114, when she left England as a child bride of eight. With her husband, Emperor Henry V, recently deceased, she was returning to England in the autumn of 1126, escorted by her father King Henry. She was virtually an alien and, yet, in the Christmas court of 1126, she was publicly named heir to the English throne and oaths of allegiance were sworn by the magnates.[44] In the various arrangements made to pave her way, her uncle, King David, played a central role. He was the first lay magnate to swear loyalty to Matilda and the symbolic value of his commitment was high.[45] The presentation of the *GRA* to her, via David, should undoubtedly be placed in this context.[46] From the perspective of the Malmesbury monks, it would have made sense to try to establish close ties with the empress by way of a historical work which her own mother, Queen Matilda, had commissioned. From David's perspective, playing intermediator might well have been a welcome tool in the, no doubt, somewhat awkward process of establishing a rapport with the female outsider who was going to be the future ruler of England and, therefore, the single most important external element affecting the future of his own kingdom. Symbolically, the book gift had potency. It introduced Matilda to the past of her future realm, just as she had been introduced to the past of the empire through a presentation copy of Ekkehard of Aura's chronicle on the occasion of her marriage to the emperor.[47] That political potency of the gift would only have been emphasised by the continuum between mother as commissioner and daughter as dedicatee.

This presentation, datable on reasonable grounds to the second half of 1126, was, from what we can tell, the beginning of the publishing history of the *GRA*. While it is theoretically possible that the work was simultaneously (or even slightly earlier) available by other means, there is no evidence to

---

[44] The story of Matilda's return is provided by Henry of Huntingdon, *Historia Anglorum*, ed. and trans. D. Greenway (Oxford: Clarendon Press, 1996) vii.37 (pp. 476–7) (henceforth, *HA*). See also Chibnall, *Empress Matilda*, pp. 50–7 and, for the wider context, Hollister, *Henry I*, pp. 313–26.

[45] Oram, *David I*, pp. 79–80.

[46] William of Malmesbury, GRA, ii.6–7 and Chibnall, *Empress Matilda*, pp. 46–7.

[47] Cambridge, Corpus Christi College, MS 373.

support the suggestion. The language of the dedicatory letter to Matilda suggests that the work had been recently finished and, indeed, the gap of time between the end of the narrative and the (probable) moment of presentation was not long.[48] More importantly, such an interpretation receives support from the manuscripts. The T version survives in nine copies, of which seven date from the twelfth or the beginning of the thirteenth century. They are all continental and, apart from one manuscript from Clairvaux, their medieval provenance is in north-eastern France or Flanders. Matilda returned to the Continent after her visit to England (1126–7) and she spent most of her time there until the end of the 1130s.[49] Given that not a single British descendant of the T manuscript presented to her is known, the odds are that she took the presentation copy to Normandy with her.[50] The dedicatory letters written for the presentation survive in only a single manuscript, from the second half of the twelfth century, now Troyes, Médiathèque du Grand Troyes, MS 294bis. This manuscript bears a late medieval Clairvaux shelfmark and, given the similarity of its mono-chromatic decoration to other Clairvaux books of the period, it appears likely that it was produced there as well.[51] The absence of the dedicatory letters from all other manuscripts suggests that the letters moved with the

---

[48] William of Malmesbury, *GRA* Ep.ii.6–7 (pp. 8–9).

[49] She appears in Rouen in May 1127 for arrangements concerning her marriage to Geoffrey, count of Anjou. Even though the wedding took place at Le Mans, in 1128, Rouen remained her principal base until 1131; see Chibnall, *Empress Matilda*, pp. 55–8.

[50] The editors suggest that the continental T version manuscripts descend from a copy sent to Matilda in Normandy (Thomson and Winterbottom, 'Introduction' (*GRA*, vol. 1), p. xv) but the course of events described above (pp. 18–22), which the editors in fact imply in their commentary volume (Thomson and Winterbottom, Commentary, *GRA* ii.7) would be the simpler hypothesis.

[51] For a description, see *Catalogue général des manuscrits des bibliothèques publiques de France. Départements*. Série in-quarto, 2 (Paris: Bibliothèque nationale de France, 1855), pp. 140–1. The decoration of Troyes 294bis finds comparison, for instance, in Troyes MSS 6 (a collection of saints' lives produced for Clairvaux) and 177 (a collection of texts on monastic spirituality).

presentation copy as separate documents, accessed by the copyists working at or for Clairvaux in the second half of the twelfth century.

If we restrict the word 'publishing' to mean the first entry of a written work into circulation with its author's permission to make more copies of it, this, then, was the instant of publication: the monastery of Malmesbury presenting William's work to Empress Matilda. However, if we think of publishing as the author–audience interface, this was just the beginning of the process. There are reasons to think that the initial book launch, despite its auspicious setting, turned out to be a disappointment. Certainly, the T manuscript given to Matilda completely failed to initiate any circulation of William's magnum opus in England, having left no textual trace in the insular transmission. The initial success on the Continent was apparently limited as well. We only find copies of the T version dating from the middle of the twelfth century onwards and they all stem from Flanders or eastern France, i.e. from outside Matilda's continental heartlands in the Rouen region and Anjou. Given that the dedicatory letters were copied at Clairvaux, it rather appears that the T manuscript started to produce off-spring only once it had, for some reason, left Matilda's orbit.

Whether William understood the disappearance of the T manuscript to the Continent as a publishing failure we cannot know but his next move certainly appears to have been an attempt to make the work more widely available by extending the publishing circle. Sometime in 1127–9 a new copy (the archetype of the second or A version) was produced from William's draft, now somewhat revised, and given to Robert, earl of Gloucester, King Henry I's influential illegitimate son. William did not explain why he had composed a new dedication but he acknowledged the previous one with his choice of words and, between the lines, one may read possible disappointment with it: 'I have thought it right to dedicate espe-cially to you (*uobis potissimum*) the *History of the English Kings* which I have lately put out (*quem nuper edidi*).'[52] The dedicatory letter is not actually found in any of the copies of the second version, only in copies of still later

---

[52] William of Malmesbury, *GRA* Ep.iii.2 (pp. 10–11). 'Hinc est quod Gesta Regum Anglorum, quae nuper edidi, uobis potissimum consecranda credidi' (trans. Winterbottom).

ones, but the epilogue of the second version makes it clear that Robert was already its dedicatee.[53] The logical conclusion is that the second presentation copy was accompanied by a physically separate cover letter, just as apparently was the case with the first one delivered to Matilda.

Manuscript evidence indicates that this presentation worked better in advancing the distribution of the work in Britain than the previous one and that its success was at least somewhat more immediate. For the second (or A) version of the *GRA*, we have ten manuscript witnesses, nine of them dating from before the middle of the thirteenth century, five from or before *c.*1200 and two probably from William's and Robert's lifetime. Apart from one manuscript described as showing English and French scribal hands, their origins have all been assigned to England.[54] While there is no evidence that would directly inform us of Robert's own contribution to this dissemination, there is evidence at least to show that William had managed to foster a close relationship with the earl. William's last historical composition, the *Historia novella*, unfinished at the time of his death, was not only dedicated to Robert but also deeply partisan towards him.[55] Furthermore, it has been plausibly suggested that the systematic toning down of material that denigrated William I and William II – Robert's grandfather and uncle – in the third version of the *GRA* resulted from Robert's feedback.[56]

---

[53] William of Malmesbury, *GRA* v.446–449 (pp. 798–801). While Robert's name is not mentioned in this passage, his identity is in no doubt. See, in particular, the passage on Robert's parentage and the explanations in Thomson and Winterbottom, *William of Malmesbury* (*GRA*, vol. 2), p. 398.

[54] Cambridge, Trinity College, MS R. 7. 10 (s. xii^{med}); London, British Library, MSS Add. 23147 (s. xii^{ex}), Arundel 35 (s. xii$^{2/4}$), Cotton Claudius C. IX (s. xiii$^{1/2}$), Harley 261 (s. xiii$^{1/4}$); Oxford, All Souls College, MS 35 (s. xiii$^{1/2}$); Oxford, Bodleian Library, MSS Hatton 54 (s. xiv^{in}), Laud Misc. 548 (s. xii/xiii); Paris, Bibliothèque nationale de France, MS lat. 6047 (s. xii/xiii), and Princeton, University Library, MS Scheide 159 (s. xiii^{ex}).

[55] See D. Crouch, 'Robert, Earl of Gloucester, and the Daughter of Zelophehad', *Journal of Medieval History*, 11 (1985), 227–43.

[56] Thomson and Winterbottom, 'Introduction', in William of Malmesbury, *Gesta Regum Anglorum: The History of the English Kings*, vol. 2, ed. R. Thomson and M. Winterbottom (Oxford: Clarendon Press, 1999), pp. xvii–xlvii, at pp. xxv–xxvi.

Most tangibly, Robert's sustained interest in William's literary activities is indicated by a manuscript that postdates both of them, London, BL, MS Royal 13 D. II, from the end of the twelfth century. This manuscript contains three texts which were dedicated to Robert: Geoffrey of Monmouth's *De gestis Britonum*, William's *GRA*, and William's *Historia novella*. They all have features indicating closeness to the dedicatee. The text of the *De gestis* is textually the single best witness of the version dedicated to Robert.[57] That of the *Historia novella* is a special 'Robertian' recension, with revisions and rubrics emphasising his achievements.[58] The text of the *GRA* is based on the third version but it has been cautiously corrected against the second version, which was the version of the presentation copy given to Robert.[59] Like the text of the *De gestis*, it too is highly accurate and has been given a prominent place in the editions. There is no independent evidence on the origin of the manuscript but its early thirteenth-century home was Margam Abbey (OCist, Glam), one of the few monastic foundations of Robert of Gloucester. The probable interpretation of this assemblage of evidence is that the book's exemplars were the presentation copies which Robert had received and which his descendants had preserved. The textual state of the *GRA* indicates that this literary patrimony contained (at least) two copies of it, i.e. both the original presentation copy with the second version text and a copy of the third version, possibly revised according to Robert's suggestions. Mainly because of the 'Robertian' nature of the text of the *Historia novella*, it has been

In the dedicatory letter to Robert, William had praised him by saying that in him 'combine the noble spirit of your grandfather, your uncle's generosity, your father's wisdom' ('cui adhesit magnanimitas aui, munificentia patrui, prudentia patris'), *GRA* Ep.iii.3 (pp. 10–11). In light of what William had actually written about these kings in his narrative, this remark could easily have been read as an ironic one.

57   M. Reeve, 'Introduction', in Geoffrey of Monmouth, *De gestis Britonum*, ed. M. Reeve, trans. N. Wright (Woodbridge: Boydell & Brewer, 2007), pp. vii–lxxvi, at p. xvi.

58   E. King, 'Introduction', in William of Malmesbury, *Historia novella*, ed. E. King (Oxford: Clarendon Press, 1998), pp. xvii–cix, at pp. lxxvii–xciv.

59   Thomson and Winterbottom, 'Introduction' (*GRA*, vol. 1), pp. xviii–xix.

suggested that it was revised by Robert's son, Roger of Worcester and, indeed, it is a possibility that all these books had belonged to him before they were used in the making of the Margam book.[60] Whether or not this was the case, the textual ensemble demonstrates that Robert took care to preserve the books he had received and that the collection was considered a patrimony worth curating by his descendants.

Manuscript evidence suggests that, from the second version onwards, the *GRA* was also being distributed from Malmesbury through other channels than Robert. One of the copies of the second version, London, British Library, MS Arundel 35, datable to William's lifetime and possibly quite close to the presentation of this version, allows us a glimpse of the mechanisms at work. Arundel 35 is textually the purest copy of the second or A version.[61] Thomson and Winterbottom have suggested that this manuscript was copied at Winchester from William's draft which had been sent there precisely for this purpose.[62] Certainly no fewer than four twelfth-century copies descend from it.[63] The contact between Malmesbury and Winchester could be framed in institutional terms but it is not difficult to name an individual who might very well have been involved. From 1129 onwards, the bishop of Winchester was Henry of Blois, to whom William was

---

[60] On Roger of Worcester's role, see King, 'Introduction', pp. xvi–xciv.

[61] See the British Library's online catalogue description: www.bl.uk/catalogues/illuminatedmanuscripts/record.asp?MSID=1641&CollID=20&NStart=35

[62] Thomson, and Winterbottom, 'Introduction' (*GRA*, vol. 2), p. xxiv and Thomson and Winterbottom, 'Introduction' (*GRA*, vol. 1), p. xv n. 12.

[63] The writing of the name of St Swithun in majuscules, at *GRA* §108, indicates a Winchester origin and later additions and the manuscript's history (see BL catalogue description) demonstrate it was used there. The initials are typical of English monastic book production of the period. The major and minor initials have foliate extensions and linear ornament in reserve. Green and red dominate the palette, while the more elaborate initial at the start, filled with foliate penwork, also has brown and pale blue. The descendants of the manuscript are Cambridge, Trinity College, MS R. 7. 10 (xii^med); London, British Library, MS Add. 23147 (xii^ex); Oxford, All Souls College, MS 35 (s. xiii^1), and Oxford, Bodleian Library, MS Laud Misc. 548 (s. xii/xiii). The Trinity and All Souls manuscripts descend from the same intermediary copy.

already connected. Henry had, since 1126, been abbot of Glastonbury, where William did much research work, and, ultimately, William dedicated his history of Glastonbury Abbey to him. What is more, we know that Henry had a copy of the *GRA* produced for the library at Glastonbury.[64]

Putting the first and second versions of the *GRA* into circulation seems to have involved at least three separate authorial distribution channels: Matilda, Robert, and Winchester. The manner of dissemination of the third (or C) version, datable to *c*.1135, suggests that, by then, this publishing circle had succeeded in creating an interest in the text. The third version survives in nine English manuscripts for which it has not been possible to establish a clear stemma. The editors have concluded that these manuscripts most likely reflect a developing exemplar, i.e. William's draft of the third version, which was copied at various moments during its composition.[65] This interpretation of the textual evidence, while it may seem audacious, finds support in the odd placement of the dedicatory epistle in these manuscripts. This is not found at the beginning of the work, which would be its natural position, but between the end of Book III and the start of Book IV.[66] Such a position seems unlikely for a copy intended to function as the official exemplar of a new version. However, in William's working copy the letter

[64] R. Sharpe, *English Benedictine Libraries: The Shorter Catalogues*. Corpus of British Medieval Library Catalogues, vol. 4 (London: British Library, 1996), B37 (pp. 160–5).

[65] See Thomson and Winterbottom, 'Introduction' (*GRA*, vol. 1), pp. xviii–xix. The C version manuscripts are Cambridge, Trinity College, collection of Prof. S. D. Keynes (AD 1411, copied by John Merylynch, monk of Glastonbury); Cambridge, University Library, MS Ii. 2. 3 (s. xii^2); London, British Library, MSS Add. 38129 (s. xv), Arundel 161 (xiv$^{1/2}$), Royal 13 D. II (s. xii^2), Royal 13 D. V (s. xiii$^{2/4}$); Oxford, All Souls College, MSS b. 32, no. 22 (two bifolia, s xii^{ex}), 33 (s. xii^2), and Paris, Bibliothèque nationale de France, MS lat. 6048 (s. xii^2). Paris, BnF, lat. 6048, which Stubbs took as being of French origin (Stubbs, 'Preface', p. lxxxvii; repeated in Thomson and Winterbottom, 'Introduction' (GRA, vol. 1) p. xviii), appears to be English, especially by its decoration; see the description in the BnF catalogue: http://archivesetmanuscrits.bnf.fr/ark:/12148/cc650714.

[66] The letter is found, so located, in all except one of the copies of the third (C) version, which are so complete that they should include it.

could easily have been placed there for practical reasons. The *GRA* consists of five books and we know from William's own testimony that there was originally a hiatus in writing after Book III was finished.[67] This kind of compositional history could have led to the draft existing as two separate codicological units, i.e. one including Books I–III and the other Books IV–V. Since the dedicatory epistle to Robert was composed later than most of the work itself, it could not be easily inserted in its proper place at the beginning of the working copy. At the same time, seeking to preserve its text on a separate leaf would have left it prone to loss. An empty leaf at the end of William's working copy would have been a natural place for making an archive copy of the dedicatory text.

Indeed, one later manuscript hints at this kind of an arrangement. Paris, Bibliothèque nationale de France, MS lat. 6048, from the second half of the twelfth century, contains a text of the third version but, untypically, omits the dedication.[68] In this manuscript, the third book, after which the dedicatory letter is found in all other copies, ends mid-page (fol. 66v), with seven ruled lines after its last words. The last word of Book III ('modum') is written in display script, an effect often reserved for the last words of a work or a codex and not used at the end of the first (fol. 7 r) or second (fol. 48 v) book of the *GRA* in this manuscript. The preface to the fourth book begins a new folio (67 r), with an elaborate initial, and the text of the fourth book itself is opened by an even grander, seven-line initial, followed by a line in extra-large display script. The other changes of books are not similarly treated.[69] This treatment of the beginning of the fourth book would be

---

[67] *GRA* iv. prol. (pp. 541–3).

[68] The BnF digital catalogue suggests a dating to the last quarter of the twelfth century (http://archivesetmanuscrits.bnf.fr/ark:/12148/cc650714) but the manuscript could equally date from the third quarter. There is no biting, except for *pp*, and capitals are not thickened or decorated with added lines. The only clear morphological traits supporting a dating late in the twelfth century are the absence of *e-caudata* and the use of a straight suspension sign.

[69] The first change, from Book I to Book II (fol. 7r), takes place just six lines from the bottom of the page, so that the initial at the start of the preface of Book II occupies the five bottom lines and the initial at the opening of the actual narrative

compatible with the exemplar having existed as two separate codices, one containing Books I–III and the other IV–V. As to the absence of a dedicatory letter in this manuscript, it bears noting that the opening folios are missing. In other words, the scribe of this manuscript may well have moved the letter to its 'correct' place at the beginning of the whole work.

Whatever the precise story behind the idiosyncratic Paris manuscript, the other representatives of the third (or C) version apparently descend from a series of copies made of William's draft of the *GRA* over the period *c.*1126–35.[70] During this period, William was working at least in part at Glastonbury, undertaking research for his work *De antiquitate ecclesiae Glastoniensis*. Traces of the Glastonbury period are observable in the content of the third version of the *GRA* as well, and the editors have suggested that it was in fact produced for the Glastonbury community.[71] Certainly, the manuscript presenting the latest state of its text was copied by a monk of Glastonbury in 1411,[72] and its exemplar was an early Glastonbury copy.

Besides being copied for the Glastonbury community in its finished state, the evolving draft of the third version was also copied during its process of composition. Most of the copies descending directly from the working copy of William's Glastonbury period are unlocalised but one of them allows us to reconstruct one of the directions in which the text travelled. This is Cambridge, University Library, MS Ii. 2. 3, from the third quarter of the twelfth century. Its medieval provenance is Buildwas

---

is found mid-page as well, on fol. 7v. The change from Book II to Book III is similar, with both initials located mid-page (fols. 48v, 49r).

[70] Thomson and Winterbottom, 'Introduction' (*GRA*, vol. 1), pp. xviii–xix.

[71] Thomson and Winterbottom, 'Introduction' (*GRA*, vol. 2), pp. xxxii–xxiii n. 25. William first added Glastonbury material to the C version but later deleted some of it, probably because it had now been published in a separate work (i.e. *De antiquitate Glastoniensis ecclesiae*).

[72] A now incomplete copy in the collection of Prof. S. D. Keynes, Trinity College, Cambridge. See Thomson and Winterbottom, 'Introduction' (*GRA*, vol. 1), p. xix. There is one potential contradiction in what Thomson and Winterbottom write. If C was 'a developing exemplar' (*ibid.*, p. xviii), it cannot at the same time have been the 'manuscript presented by William to Glastonbury' (*ibid.*, p. xix), unless William deposited his own working copy in the library.

(OCist, Salop) and it has elaborate monochromatic initials, often found in Cistercian books of the period, although these are unique in their decorative language. It was very likely produced for the Buildwas library around 1170.[73] However, its text has an interpolated passage, which led William Stubbs, the nineteenth-century editor of the *GRA*, to think that it was made for St Peter's Abbey, Gloucester.[74] This passage narrates how a certain Roger of Gloucester donated a manor to St Peter's on his deathbed and it additionally contains the text of the donation document and a later court decision defending St Peter's title to this manor.[75] While St Peter's was not the place of origin for this manuscript, Stubbs was correct in assuming that the *text* of the *GRA* with such an interpolation must have been originally made for use at St Peter's. The most plausible explanation for the presence of this passage in the Buildwas book (CUL Ii. 2. 3) is that it was copied from an exemplar belonging to St Peter's. Two as yet unlocalised twelfth-century copies, Oxford, All Souls College, fragment b. 32, no. 22 (two bifolia) and Oxford, All Souls College, MS 33 also contain the interpolation and, thus, descend from the same St Peter's copy. St Peter's Abbey, renovated under its post-Conquest abbot, Serlo (d. 1104), was flourishing in William's time and its book collection evidently functioned as another important supply centre for the *GRA*, although whether William was directly involved in making the text available at Gloucester is difficult to know. However, the fact that William's unfinished text was copied several times during the Glastonbury period indicates that the *GRA* was now subject to considerable attention. One suspects that the extension of William's publishing circle to include Robert of Gloucester, Henry of Blois, and the Winchester and Glastonbury communities, two focal points in the ecclesiastical landscape of south-western England, was an important factor in its increasing appeal.[76]

---

[73] J. M. Sheppard, *The Buildwas Books: Book Production, Acquisition and Use at an English Cistercian Monastery, 1165–c.1400* (Oxford: The Oxford Bibliographical Society, 1996), pp. 34–9.

[74] Stubbs, 'Preface', p. lxxxvi. [75] *GRA* v.398.4 (pp. 830–3).

[76] For the great wealth and centrality of Glastonbury, see N. E. Stacy, 'Henry of Blois and the Lordship of Glastonbury', *The English Historical Review*, 114 (1999), 1–33.

Finally, the third, or 'Glastonbury', version was followed by the fourth (B) version of the *GRA*. In this version, from which the most critical comments on Robert of Gloucester's ancestors had been purged, the dedication to him was finally placed in its logical place at the beginning of the work. The textual history shows us that a new master copy had now been made and one suspects it was delivered to Robert. There is, however, little evidence as to the contemporary distribution of the fourth version. It exists in eight manuscripts but, compared to the previous versions, more of these are relatively late copies, the two earliest (unprovenanced) manuscripts datable to the last quarter of the twelfth century.[77] At this stage, the *GRA* was already available through many channels and, perhaps also because the latest version did not add to its chronological coverage, it did not come to enjoy any privileged position in the later dissemination.

The story of how the *GRA* entered circulation thus consists of two discrete moments of publishing, in which the author took the initiative, first by delivering a copy to Empress Matilda via King David and then by giving another one to Robert of Gloucester. The dedications, however, show us only one part of William's publishing circle. The cathedral priory of Winchester and Glastonbury abbey functioned as important textual supply points already during the period of William's literary activity and their involvement in the distribution was very likely connected to Henry of Blois's interest in William's work. While the text of course spread in a more organic way once it was widely enough available, the first stages in the distribution process suggest that the authorial publishing circle was important in creating this initial availability.

The workings of the publishing circle are highlighted by a comparison with William's other main work, *Gesta pontificum Anglorum* (*GPA*). While the *GPA* is in some sense the ecclesiastical counterpart of the *GRA*, there were fundamental differences between the two projects. Written over a short period time – perhaps two or three years – the *GPA* is a less polished literary product than the *GRA*. Moreover, it never received any dedication

---

[77] London, British Library, MS Royal 13 B. XIX and Philadelphia, Free Library, MS Lewis E. 247.

and its prefatory material is less comprehensive than that of the *GRA*.[78] The *GPA*, a conspectus of the English church and especially of its 'monastic wing', was apparently never formally published, perhaps because it was difficult to think of single dedicatee for such a work. This was William writing about and for his own people, the monastic communities of England.

The textual transmission indicates that the early distribution of this text happened differently to that of the *GRA*, according to a process that would appear to have been fortuitous rather than planned. The *GPA* exists in two different versions. The first branch of the transmission went back to a single copy of William's draft. It is preserved in six manuscripts, of which all but one are known to have belonged to religious institutions in Yorkshire or Lincolnshire. It has been plausibly suggested that they originated from a copy made of an early state of the *GPA* for some northern house.[79] This first version included curiously offensive material and was soon (*c*.1134) thoroughly revised by William.[80] Most likely, it was never intended for wide circulation and its distribution in Yorkshire seems, from an authorial

---

[78] See R. M. Thomson, 'Introduction', in William of Malmesbury, *Gesta Pontificum Anglorum. The History of the English Bishops*, vol. 2 (Oxford: Clarendon Press, 2007), pp. xix–liii, at p. xxi.

[79] See M. Winterbottom, 'Introduction', in William of Malmesbury, *Gesta Pontificum Anglorum. The History of the English Bishops*, vol. 1 (Oxford: Clarendon Press, 2007), pp. xi–xxxi, at pp. xiii–xiv. The manuscripts of the beta group are London, British Library, MSS Cotton Claudius A. V (s. xii, Belvoir priory, OSB, Lincs), Harley 3641 (s. xii[ex], Byland abbey, OCist, Yorks), Harley 2 (s. xiii[in], Thornton priory, OSA, Lincs); Oxford, Bodleian Library, MSS Bodley 357 (s. xii, Bridlington priory, OSA, Yorks ER), Rawlinson B. 199 (s. xiv–xv, York Minster), and Laud Misc. 598 (s. xv, medieval provenance unknown).

[80] This work of suppression, which took place *c*.1134, constitutes the one clear textual divide in the history of the *GPA*. See Thomson, 'Introduction' (*GPA*, vol. 2), pp. xxiv–xxv. William's working copy, Oxford, Magdalen College, MS lat. 172, has been preserved, and the systematic nature of the work of revision is visible in this manuscript. It was not the original draft but a clean working copy made by William himself. See Winterbottom, 'Introduction' (*GPA*, vol. 1), pp. xi–xii.

perspective, like an accident, perhaps the result of a draft given to another for comment and then unintentionally entering wider circulation.

Interestingly enough, we do not find a clear final state of the second version either. Just as was the case with the third version of the *GRA*, we encounter a textual spectrum resulting from copies having been made of the evolving draft at various stages in its development.[81] Some of the manuscripts of the second version fall into geographical groupings. The members of one belonged to religious houses in the Midlands and Yorkshire,[82] and those of another have associations with Kentish institutions.[83] The impression is that William never issued a finished master copy of the *GPA* but that some monastic houses, once they knew about his project, arranged for the copying of his working copy and then passed on the text within their own circle. A text that was intended primarily for readers based in religious houses and cathedral chapters perhaps did not need promotion in the same way as one that sought more widespread and mixed readership in the twelfth-century *res publica litterarum*, aristocratic and scholarly circles included. In other words, the monastic publishing framework functioned, for certain kinds of texts, so efficiently that it was not in equal measure necessary to actively create a publishing circle to achieve distribution.

3 Henry of Huntingdon

William may have travelled across Britain in search of sources but he remained a monk, whose life unfolded within the stable framework of a Benedictine community. Henry of Huntingdon (*c*.1088–1157) played

---

[81] Thomson, 'Introduction' (*GPA*, vol. 2), pp. xxxiii–xxxv and Winterbottom, 'Introduction' (*GPA*, vol. 1), pp. xiii–xv.

[82] London, British Library, MS Royal 13 D. V (s. xiii, St Albans abbey, OSB, Herts); Oxford, Bodleian Library, MS Bodley 956 (s. xv[in], Lichfield Cathedral); Cambridge, Trinity College, MS R. 5. 40 (s. xiii, York Minster), and Cambridge, Corpus Christi College, MS 43 (s. xiv, East Anglia).

[83] London, British Library, MS Harley 261 (s. xiii, Rochester Cathedral Priory); Oxford, Bodleian Library, MS Hatton 54 (s. xiv[in], likewise Rochester), and Cambridge, University Library, MS Ff. i. 25 (s. xii, medieval provenance unknown).

many more varied roles in his life. Son of the archdeacon of Huntingdon, he received a superb Latin education at Lincoln, where he was a member of the glittering episcopal curia of Robert Bloet (d. 1123). In Robert's entourage, he also frequented Henry I's court (during *c.*1120–3) and very likely had aspirations towards being a court poet. However, Robert's fall from grace, in 1123, seems to have cut this career short and, for the remainder of his days, Henry was to be archdeacon of Huntingdon, a position he had inherited from his father in 1110. Over the years, Henry also married, had children, and managed his family estate.[84]

Alongside his duties and other activities, all through his life Henry wrote. He produced love poems, epigrams, a herbal, a lapidary, epistles, and what undoubtedly was his life's central literary project, the *Historia Anglorum* (*HA*), a history of the English people from their first arrival in Britain until Henry's own time.[85] Whereas some of Henry's works do not survive at all, and others do so in only a small number of copies, the *HA* is preserved in around forty medieval manuscripts, of which thirteen can be dated to the twelfth century (including manuscripts dated to the turn of the century).

[84] For Henry of Huntingdon's life, see D. Greenway, 'Henry [Henry of Huntingdon] (c. 1088–c. 1157), Historian and Poet', *Oxford Dictionary of National Biography*, https://doi-org.libproxy.helsinki.fi/10.1093/ref:odnb/12970, accessed 4 April 2018 and J. Gillingham, 'Henry of Huntingdon in His Time (1135) and Place (between Lincoln and the Royal Court)', in K. Stopka (ed.), *Gallus Anonymous and His Chronicle in the Context of Twelfth-Century Historiography from the Perspective of the Latest Research* (Crakow: Polish Academy of Arts and Sciences, 2010), pp. 157–72.

[85] For Henry's literary production, see Greenway, 'Introduction', pp. cxii–cxv; A. G. Rigg, 'Henry of Huntingdon's Herbal', *Mediaeval Studies*, 65 (2003), 213–92; D. Greenway, 'Henry of Huntingdon as Poet: The De Herbis Rediscovered', *Medium Aevum*, 74 (2005), 329–32; W. Black, 'Henry of Huntingdon's Lapidary Rediscovered and His Anglicanus Ortus Reassembled', *Mediaeval Studies*, 68 (2006), 43–88, and Henry of Huntingdon, *Anglicanus ortus: A Verse Herbal of the Twelfth Century*, ed. by W. Black (Toronto: Pontifical Institute of Mediaeval Studies, 2012).

At a glance, the publishing history of this moderately successful work might look simpler than that of William's *GRA*. In all those manuscripts that include the prologue (and these are the great majority), the *HA* is dedicated to the same person, Alexander, bishop of Lincoln (d. 1148), Henry's superior in the ecclesiastical hierarchy and successor to his first protector, Robert Bloet. Indeed, it was Alexander, Henry tells us, who had commanded him to compose the history.[86] Besides a single patron, Henry also gives us a single date for the completion of the work, the year 1135, about which he wrote at some length in the epilogue of the *HA*:

> This is the year which contains the writer. The thirty-fifth year of the reign of the glorious and invincible Henry, king of the English. The sixty-ninth year from the arrival in England in our own time, of the supreme Norman race. The 703rd year from the coming of the English into England. The 2265th year from the coming of the Britons to settle in the same island. The 5317th year from the beginning of the world. The 1135th year of grace. This, then is the year from which the writer of the *History* wished his age to be reckoned by posterity.[87]

Laying such emphasis on the date of writing is quite extraordinary, as John Gillingham has noted.[88] As if this were not enough, in several of the

---

[86] Henry of Huntingdon, *HA* Prol. (pp. 4–7); see also Greenway, 'Introduction', p. lxvii.

[87] Henry of Huntingdon, *HA* viii.Epil.1–2 (pp. 494–5). 'Hic est annus qui comprehendit scriptorem. Annus tricesimus quintus regni gloriosi inuictissimi regis Anglorum Henrici. Annus lxix ab aduentu Normannorum gentis temporibus excellentissime nostris in Angliam. Annus ab aduentu Anglorum in Angliam dcciii. Annus ab aduentu Britannorum ad hanc eandem insulam inhabitandam ii M et cc et lxv. Annus ab initio mundi v M et ccc et xvii. Annus gratie Mcxxxv. Hic est igitur annus ille a quo scriptor historie suam uoluit etatem a sequentibus computari' (trans. Greenway).

[88] Gillingham, 'Henry of Huntingdon in His Time', pp. 160–1.

manuscripts this date also appears as a colophon and as an introductory rubric, both apparently autograph.[89]

Henry's words, however, conceal, quite intentionally, a complicated history of composition and publication. Diana Greenway, the text's modern editor, has identified no fewer than six different versions which entered circulation at various dates, none of them ending in 1135 and none of them necessarily even published that year.[90] In earlier scholarship, these versions were labelled as 'editions',[91] a term abandoned by Greenway in preference for the more neutral word 'version', since, as she rightly points out, 'the different forms of Henry's text are not polished "editions" in the modern sense: rather, they reproduce his work at particular stages in its evolution, when copies were made.'[92] However, while some of the six versions did not result from intentional publication, others certainly did. An examination of the genesis of these different versions demonstrates that the process of publishing was, in Henry's case, intimately linked to advancing the distribution of the text.

To understand this story, we need to start from the two earliest versions of the *HA* known to us – versions which show us a still unpublished text. The first thing to observe is indeed that Henry withheld finishing and publishing the *HA* for a long time. Whereas the chronological narrative of the first version ends at 1129, it contains references to events which took place later, in 1131 and 1133. These have been interpreted by Greenway, plausibly, as later additions made to the margins of a draft whose writing had concluded in 1129 or 1130.[93] The second version in other respects

---

[89] In some manuscripts, the colophon was changed to 1145, apparently because the scribe observed that the narrative does not in fact end in 1135. On the colophons, see B. Pohl, 'When Did Robert of Torigni First Receive Henry of Huntingdon's Historia Anglorum, and Why Does It Matter?', *The Haskins Society Journal*, 26 (2015), 143–68, at pp. 154–7, 167.

[90] Summarised in Greenway, 'Introduction', pp. lxviii–lxix, table 2.

[91] See T. Arnold, 'Introduction', in *Henrici Archidiaconi Huntendunensis Historia Anglorum*, Rolls Series 74, ed. T. Arnold (London: Longman & Co., 1879), pp. i–lxvi, at pp. xi–xvi and F. Liebermann, 'Heinrich von Huntingdon', Forschungen Zur Deutschen Geschichte, 18 (1878), 265–95, at 272–90.

[92] Greenway, 'Introduction', p. lxvii.   [93] Ibid., pp. lxvii–lxx.

resembles exactly the first but it contains an added epilogue which explicitly dates the composition to 1135.[94] Each version is preserved in one twelfth-century copy and neither of these manuscripts was copied from a finished exemplar. The first version, found in Edinburgh, National Library of Scotland, MS Advocates' 33.5.4 lacks rubrics, the so-called *laudes* of the Roman emperors (which constituted the first book of the *HA* in its finished state) and it also lacks the epilogue.[95] The *laudes* and the epilogue, but not the rubrics or the prologue, are found in the one twelfth-century witness of the second version, Aberystwyth, NLW, MS Peniarth 382, copied *c*.1196. As Diana Greenway has demonstrated, this manuscript descends from an intermediary manuscript copied while Henry was still at work.[96]

In other words, what evidence we have for the earliest distribution suggests that Henry, first, sat on an essentially completed work for the

---

[94] Certain features of the epilogue further suggest that it had been originally drafted in 1129. See *ibid.*, pp. cxlvii–cxlviii.

[95] The Edinburgh manuscript has been previously dated to the middle of the twelfth century, but on palaeographical grounds the possibility it was produced earlier, in the 1130s, perhaps copying directly from Henry's autograph, cannot be excluded. The text is written in an early praegothic script, using ampersand, *e-caudata*, and both forms of *d*. Feet of minims have horizontal ticks. No bitings, not even that of *pp*, are to be seen and round *s* is not used. Tall *s* frequently descends below the baseline. Initials mostly use a single colour, in simple Romanesque shapes. A small number of minor initials have pen flourishes in green and blue. These seem later than the script and may well be later additions, probably made while the continuation of the text was copied in the second half of the twelfth century, since a similar green is used in this part of the manuscript. The diacritic signs, which appear systematically in some parts of the text and may make the manuscript seem rather late at first glance, were added *c*.1300, when the manuscript was heavily annotated. This can be deduced from the way the ink of these signs mirrors the ink of the marginalia; see, for instance, fols. 6r and 8r.

[96] In other words, the Peniarth manuscript reflects Henry's draft at an updated state, after the addition of the *laudes*; see Greenway, 'Introduction', pp. lxvi–lxx. The manuscript was apparently owned by a person referring to himself as Edmund the Chaplain in 1196. This is suggested by a series of datings (fol. 42v, margin), all pointing to AD 1196, in a hand different from the text but probably not much later, ending 'a natiuitate Edmundi capellani 64, ab ordinatione ipsius 33'.

period 1129–33/5 and then it was in some way made available as essentially unfinished (versions one and two). The imperfect state of the preserved copies of these versions suggests that this initial circulation was limited. The presence of the epilogue with the date of composition in the second version does not imply otherwise. While it used to be assumed that the epilogue would fix the date of 'official' publication to 1135, Greenway's and Benjamin Pohl's more recent studies have refuted this idea.[97] Greenway's examination of the textual history has demonstrated that the Peniarth manuscript (the sole witness of the second version) descends from the same draft as the Advocates manuscript (the sole witness of the first version), simply representing the authorial draft in an updated state. However, the mass of manuscripts with the 1135 epilogue represent completely different, later, and more polished textual states.[98] What is more, the previously held proposition that Robert of Torigni would have had access to a version published in 1135 has been thoroughly discredited by Benjamin Pohl's reconsideration of Robert's use of the *HA*. We can now be certain that Robert only had recourse to one of the later versions.

Admittedly, Henry's *HA* was not completely unavailable in *c*.1135. Geoffrey of Monmouth, who likewise belonged to the literary circle around Henry's patron Alexander, had access to the *HA*, most likely sometime between 1135 and 1137.[99] The manuscripts of the first two versions of the *HA* themselves, moreover, constitute evidence of limited circulation taking place in the 1130s. The most obvious case is that of the Edinburgh manuscript, which, as discussed above, does seem to belong to this period. However, we have also observed that these manuscripts represent an unfinished work and we know that when Henry went to Le Bec in January 1139 he did not give Robert of Torigni a copy, even though he must have known that Robert was a keen collector (and distributor) of historical works. This visit to Le Bec,

---

[97] Greenway, 'Introduction', pp. lxxii–lxxiii and Pohl, 'When Did Robert of Torigni', *passim*.

[98] D. Greenway, 'Henry of Huntingdon and the Manuscripts of his Historia Anglorum', *Anglo-Norman Studies*, 11 (1987), 103–26, at 107 n. 29 and Greenway, 'Introduction', pp. lxvii–lxx.

[99] See Tatlock, *The Legendary History of Britain*, pp. 34, 67, 121, 281.

moreover, occasioned a curious document which perfectly fits the idea that the *HA* was essentially still a work in progress in early 1139. Robert of Torigni introduced Henry to Geoffrey of Monmouth's *De gestis Britonum*, previously unknown to him, and Henry wrote about this discovery to a person called Warin the Briton.[100] Much later, Robert included the same letter in his own chronicle, with a preface that underlined his own role in making Geoffrey's work available to Henry. In this preface, he mentioned how he had inquired of Henry on this occasion about the *HA*, which shows that he was interested in Henry's activities and suggests that a copy of the *HA* was not available at their meeting. The content and purpose of Henry's letter point to similar conclusions. The letter was addressed to Warin who, it is stated, had commented on the *HA*, in particular wondering why it had nothing to tell about the early British kings. The fact of his having written a long letter, running to twelve and a half pages in the printed edition, demonstrates that Henry valued Warin's opinion and indicates close personal contact between the two. This kind of exchange would be well accounted for if Warin had been part of a small circle to whom Henry had made the work available for comment. While reliable identification is not possible, one of Henry's contemporaries at Lincoln may have been a certain Guarinus the canon.[101] Certainly, the scholarly community around Lincoln Cathedral, where Henry himself had studied and to which he maintained very close links, would be prime territory for that sort of limited early circulation.

Whatever the precise extent and context of the preliminary distribution of the *HA* in the 1130s, it is clear that, early in the 1140s, the status of the *HA* changed. The next – the so-called third – version of the *HA* continued the chronological narrative up to Christmas 1138; its writing finished in 1141 or 1142.[102] For this version, the state of the text, its paratexts, and the

---

[100] The letter is preserved in the manuscripts of the *HA* and of Robert's *Chronicle*. It has been edited by Greenway in Henry of Huntingdon, *HA*, pp. 558–83. For its substance, see Wright, 'The Place of Henry of Huntingdon's *Epistola ad Warinum*'.

[101] See Henry of Huntingdon, *HA*, p. 559 n. 2 and *Fasti Ecclesiae Anglicanae 1066–1300, vol. 3, Lincoln* (London: Institute of Historical Research, 1977), p. 147.

[102] For the date of writing, see Greenway, 'Introduction', p. lxxii.

manuscripts all join forces to give an impression of a work thoroughly polished and duly published. Whereas the two previous versions, each surviving in single twelfth-century manuscripts, were copied directly from Henry's evolving autograph, all the manuscripts of the third version descend from a common source that was different from the autograph – the presentation copy, one may logically presume.[103] By now, the *laudes* had been integrated into the text, it had received rubrication, and a colophon had been added. The two earliest manuscripts have an introductory rubric as well.[104] The number of manuscripts witnessing only parts of the third version (6) is double the number of manuscripts of the two previous versions put together (3), which also suggests wider circulation.[105]

Only now, more than ten years after the main narrative had been completed, Henry took the necessary steps to create a finished literary product of the *HA* and put it into open circulation – all the while keeping up the appearance that the work had been written in 1135. 'This is the year which contains the writer', he stated, and '[t]his, then is the year from which the writer of the *History* wished his age to be reckoned by posterity'.[106] Why such a delay and why such an emphasis on the year of writing? Henry's hesitation in publishing and his decision to obscure the date of composition had to do with his handling of his portrait of King Henry I. As Alan Cooper has demonstrated, a series of modifications turned the relatively favourable portrait of the first two versions – written while the king was alive – into

---

[103] *Ibid.*, pp. lxvi–lxxi.

[104] London, British Library, MS Egerton 3668, fols. 1r–147r (s. xii^med) and Cambridge, Corpus Christi College, MS 281 (s. xii²). The rubric repeats 1135 as the year of writing: 'Incipit prologus historie Anglorum contexta ab Henrico Huntudonensi archidiacono anno gratie 1135.'

[105] Cambridge, Corpus Christi College, MS 280 (s. xii²); Durham, Ushaw College, MS 6 (s. xii²); Edinburgh, NLS, MS Advocates 33.5.4, fols. 1–82 (as a s. xii² continuation to the first version, from s. xii^med); Glasgow, University Library, MS Hunter U.6.6 (s. xiv^{1/2}); London, British Library, MS Add. 24061 (xiv^{1/2}), and MS Egerton 3668, fols. 1r–147r (s. xii^med).

[106] Henry of Huntingdon, *HA*, viii.Epil.1–2 (pp. 494–5). 'Hic est annus qui comprehendit scriptorem. ... Hic est igitur annus ille a quo scriptor historie suam uoluit etatem a sequentibus computari' (trans. Greenway).

a brutally critical one in the third.[107] Furthermore, the king's cruelty and wilfulness were underlined in the *De contemptu mundi* letter, now integrated into the *HA*, which also showed the king scheming to bring down Robert Bloet – Henry of Huntingdon's own link to the court in the golden days of his youth.[108] The character assassination was completed by the newly written tenth book of the *HA*, which included a new, damning portrait and the oft-cited description of the king's disintegrating corpse.[109] Henry of Huntingdon was, of course, aware that he could be accused of hypocrisy in having changed his view of King Henry and he discussed this accusation explicitly in *De contemptu mundi*, finding various excuses.[110] The obfuscation of the date of writing was undoubtedly one part of his authorial strategy of defence: it created the appearance that the work had been finished within the king's lifetime.

While we have no independent evidence on the precise circumstances of the publication of the *HA* in 1141 or 1142, the most obvious procedure

---

[107] A. Cooper, '"The Feet of Those That Bark Shall Be Cut Off": Timorous Historians and the Personality of Henry I', *Anglo-Norman Studies*, 23 (2000), 47–67, at 48–51. Henry was given a generic and puffed-up epitaph, very different from the others found in the *HA*, and Cooper and Gillingham are surely right in interpreting it as an ironic one; see Cooper, '"The Feet of Those That Bark"', 49 and Gillingham, 'Henry of Huntingdon in His Time', p. 166.

[108] Henry of Huntingdon, *HA De cont.*12 (pp. 604–5), 'Unde dicitur, "regia res scelus est." Rex Henricus fratrem suum et dominum Robertum in carcerem perhennem posuit, et usque dum moreretur detinuit. Neptum suarum oculos erui fecit, multos prodicione cepit, multos subdole interfecit, multa contra sacramenta egit. Semper cupiditati et auaricie deseruiuit' (trans. Greenway).

[109] Henry of Huntingdon, *HA* x.1–2 (pp. 698–705). Other modifications also tried to give the impression that Henry had composed the work while the king was alive. Most blatantly, Henry included a long letter purportedly written to Henry I but containing references to events which took place only after his death; see Greenway, 'Introduction', p. lxxii. One cannot but agree with Cooper's judgement that '[i]n Henry of Huntingdon's work, the contrast between the opinions expressed during the king's lifetime and those expressed after his death could not be more pointed'; Cooper, '"The Feet of Those That Bark"', 49.

[110] Gillingham, 'Henry of Huntingdon in His Time', pp. 166–7.

would have been to present a copy of the finished work to Alexander of Lincoln, by whom the *HA* had originally been commissioned – a very long time ago by this point. This presentation did not, however, lead to any very wide dissemination. The number of manuscripts of the third version (6), while bigger than that of the first (1) or second (2) versions, is not high if compared to the more successful versions of William's *GRA*, let alone Geoffrey of Monmouth's *De gestis Britonum*, and a number of details renders it still less impressive. While four of the witnesses date from the twelfth century, only two of them, Egerton 3668 and CCCC 280, faithfully reproduce the whole third version. One of the partial witnesses is the Advocates copy of the *first* version, into which the new chronological coverage provided by the third version was simply added. In other words, we see a copy stemming from the period of limited circulation, and possibly from Henry's closest circles, being updated. The other is Ushaw College, MS 6, an idiosyncratic Yorkshire amalgam integrating Henry's work with Geoffrey's *De gestis*.[111] Moreover, the earlier of the two faithful copies, one contemporary with Henry – Egerton 3668 – was corrected against the master copy of the *next* version, i.e. the fourth, which, we know, travelled to France soon after its making.[112] This indicates that the Egerton manuscript remained close to Henry, perhaps in Lincoln. The manuscript evidence for successful distribution of the third version of the *HA* as a self-standing literary work thus almost completely disintegrates when interrogated in detail.

The slow take-off of the circulation of the now, nevertheless, undoubtedly published *HA* may have been one reason why Henry kept on seeking new avenues for its distribution. Over the next few years, he created a fourth version, which saw stylistic improvement throughout the narrative and took the story chronologically to 1146. It ended with King Stephen's crown-wearing in Lincoln at Christmas in that year, an event at which Henry himself was present. This ceremony symbolised the normalisation of the relationship between King Stephen and Alexander of Lincoln, providing a suitable place

---

[111] Durham, Ushaw College, MS 6 (s. xii²) and Edinburgh, National Library of Scotland, MS Advocates 33.5.4 (s. xii^med).

[112] Egerton 3668 was in Durham Cathedral Priory in the early thirteenth century and, while its origin remains unknown, one might suspect Lincoln itself.

for a halt in the narrative. The textual history shows that a complete new master copy (delta) was now produced from Henry's draft, just as was done when the third version was finished.[113] The logical assumption that delta was also a presentation manuscript given to the patron, Alexander of Lincoln, is compatible with what textual history tells us about its movements. First, delta was used to correct the Egerton manuscript (possibly in Lincoln) and that is the only direct textual trace of it in England. Very soon afterwards it travelled to Normandy, where a new recension was produced out of it by Robert of Torigni, then prior of Le Bec.[114] All surviving descendants of delta belong to this recension, called beta by the editor. The movement of delta parallels the itinerary of Alexander of Lincoln, who travelled to meet the pope in Auxerre in August 1147, just after the fourth version had been finished.[115] Le Bec would not have been a surprising stopover on such a journey.

As to how precisely Robert of Torigni gained access to the text of the fourth version, two scenarios suggest themselves. Either he had a copy made of the presentation copy delta or delta itself ended up in his hands. The latter proposition receives support from the manuscript evidence. On the Continent, the revised delta quickly gave rise to two new manuscripts. These are its earliest surviving descendants, Paris, Bibliothèque nationale de France, MS lat. 6042 and Cambridge, University Library, MS Gg. 2. 21, both dated to the 1150s.[116] The Paris manuscript was demonstrably used by Robert of Torigni himself and the Cambridge one belonged to Philip, bishop of Bayeux.[117] Patricia Stirnemann has noted that the two first initials

[113] Greenway, 'Introduction', pp. cxviii (table 3), cxxix–cxxx, and cxlvii–clii.

[114] *Ibid.*, p. lxxv and pp. cli–clii.

[115] Henry of Huntingdon, *HA* x.25 (pp. 750–1). See Greenway, 'Introduction', pp. lv–lvi.

[116] On the dating, see the discussion in P. Stirnemann, 'Two Twelfth-Century Bibliophiles and Henry of Huntingdon's *Historia Anglorum*', *Viator*, 24 (1993), 121–42, at 137.

[117] L. Delisle, 'Préface', in *Chronique de Robert de Torigni* (Rouen: A. Le Brument, 1872), pp. i–lxxi, at pp. lv–lxi; Stirnemann, 'Two Twelfth-Century Bibliophiles', 135; Pohl, 'When Did Robert of Torigni'.

of the Paris manuscript (C on fol. 3r, B on fol. 4r) show decorative motifs that are of English origin and unknown in continental manuscripts of the period. At the same time, the illuminator's native decorative idiom was continental and, indeed, he may have been the same draughtsman who decorated two other manuscripts produced close to Robert of Torigni. By this reckoning, Stirnemann has concluded that the source of the designs was most probably an insular exemplar.[118] This is compatible with the hypothesis that the exemplar was the presentation copy, received from Alexander and revised by Robert. In addition, the structure and the motifs of the insular-influenced initial 'C', which begins the prologue in the Paris manuscript, find close parallel in the much less well executed initial 'C' found in the earliest of all the manuscripts of the *HA*, the Advocates manuscript of the first version.[119] It is a possibility that both manuscripts echo styles current in Lincoln at the time.

At the same time, it is clear that the Paris manuscript, certainly used by Robert, could not have been the first copy in his possession. It is already a fair copy of the text as revised by Robert. In other words, Robert's changes and interpolations were drafted somewhere else – probably in the margins of the exemplar, which is known to have been his approach with other manuscripts. What is more, both the Paris and the Cambridge manuscripts are densely annotated with distinctive 'a' and 'N' annotations, very likely to have been copied from the exemplar since their distribution in the two manuscripts is near identical. Similar, and similarly dense, annotations are found in a well-known manuscript that was certainly copied under Robert's supervision and revised by him – Leiden, Universiteitsbibliotheek, MS BPL 20. In this manuscript, it can be demonstrated that the annotations are, indeed, in Robert's own hand.[120] The close similarity of the annotations

---

[118] Stirnemann, 'Two Twelfth-Century Bibliophiles', 123, 127. The manuscripts possibly decorated by the same artist are Leiden, Universiteitsbibliotheek, MS BPL 20 and Avranches, Bibliothèque municipale, MS 159.

[119] Edinburgh, NLS, MS Advocates' 33.5.4, fol. 1r.

[120] Robert's involvement in the production of the Leiden manuscript has long been suspected and is confirmed by Benjamin Pohl; see B. Pohl, '"Abbas qui et scriptor?": The Handwriting of Robert of Torigni and his Scribal Activity as

in the Paris and Cambridge manuscripts to those of the Leiden manuscript, certainly made by Robert, indicates that their exemplar was also a manuscript annotated by Robert personally. Set alongside the art-historical evidence, the most economical explanation is that the exemplar was the presentation copy delta itself, which Robert had interpolated and marked up.

In addition to the Paris and Cambridge manuscripts, two other twelfth-century copies descend from Robert's recension. It (or a lost intermediary) was used as the exemplar in the copying of a historical compilation, Rouen, Bibliothèque municipale, MS U.74 (1177), for the library of Jumièges, at the very end of the twelfth century.[121] Perhaps more surprisingly, this circulated back to England, as is evinced by London, Lambeth Palace, MS 327, (fols. 1r–176r, s. xii$^{2/2}$). This manuscript has a fifteenth- or sixteenth-century *ex libris* of the Augustinian priory of Bourne in Lincolnshire and its decoration, script, and the placement of a list of the archbishops of Canterbury as the first item in the codex would all indicate an English

---

Abbot of Mont-Saint-Michel (1154–1186)', *Traditio*, 69 (2014), 45–86. As Pohl explains, Robert did not copy any of the works found in the manuscript himself but the whole was corrected and annotated by him. Pohl does not provide explicit discussion of the monograms but they are in the same hue of ink as the textual notes which Pohl identifies as being in Robert's hand and morphologically identical to the monograms of BnF lat. 6042 and CUL Gg. 2. 21.

[121] The manuscript has a (?)thirteenth-century Jumièges ex libris. Palaeographical comparison with other Jumièges manuscripts confirms that it was produced for the monastery. U.74 is entirely the work of the same scribe who copied fols. 2r–111r and 178rb–194v of Rouen, BM, MS U 102 (containing saints' lives belonging to the Jumièges reading cycle) and the codicological unit constituting the core of Rouen, BM, MS Y 15 (starting on 13r), containing the Eusebius-Jerome chronicle. The distinctive decoration, found in all twelfth-century codicological units of these manuscripts, is also by the same artist, who may be identical with the main scribe. On the exemplars of the Rouen manuscripts, see D. N. Dumville, 'An Early Text of Geoffrey of Monmouth's *Historia Regum Britanniae* and the Circulation of Some Latin Histories in Twelfth-Century Normandy', *Arthurian Literature* 4 (1985), 1–36, at 7.

origin.[122] In terms of advancing the distribution, the inclusion of Robert of Torigni in Henry's publishing circle proved in this way to be very beneficial. It is most likely that Henry had agreed with Alexander that he make the text available to Robert, in the hope that Robert would show the *HA* to others, just as he had shown Geoffrey's *De gestis Britonum* to Henry.

Having run this errand for Henry, Alexander of Lincoln died in February 1148, of a disease he had acquired on his continental journey.[123] Henry's publishing activities were, however, far from over. He immediately went back to working on the *HA*, creating the so-called fifth version, which extended the narrative to the ascent of Alexander's successor, Robert de Chesney (6 January 1149). Although this version retained the earlier dedication to Alexander, and still purported 1135 to be the year of writing, it is highly likely that a presentation copy of it was given to bishop Robert, as Greenway has suggested.[124] The fifth version gained popularity over time. There exist three copies from the turn of the twelfth and thirteenth centuries and three others from the first half of the thirteenth, all of which are almost certainly of insular origin.[125] Given that it provided more extensive chronological coverage, it was likely to be preferred over the earlier versions as time passed. However, there is less manuscript evidence on its immediate distribution during Henry's lifetime than is the case with the previous versions, of which we have at least some contemporary copies. The impression is that, despite the relaunch, the work was still not as

[122] In Cambridge, UL, MS Gg. 2. 21 the bishops' lists begin with Le Mans, in BnF lat. 6042 with Rouen.

[123] Henry of Huntingdon, *HA* x.25 (pp. 750–1).

[124] Greenway, 'Introduction', pp. lxxv–lxxvi.

[125] Paris, Bibliothèque nationale de France, MS lat. 10185 (s. xii/xiii); Oxford, Bodleian Library, MS Laud Misc. 564 (s. xii/xiii); Stonyhurst, Stonyhurst College, MS 26 (s. xii/xiii); London, Lambeth Palace, MS 179 (s. xiii), London, BL, MS Arundel 48 (s. xiii$^{1/2}$), and Baltimore, Walters Art Gallery, MS W 793 (s. xiii$^{1/2}$). Paris, BnF, MS lat. 10185 travelled to Saint-Denis early on but palaeographically and by its contents an insular origin appears very likely. Patricia Stirnemann has suggested it may have been brought to Saint-Denis by its Scottish abbot, Henry Troon (1204–17/18). See Stirnemann, 'Two Twelfth-Century Bibliophiles', 121 n. 2.

effectively distributed as those of William of Malmesbury or, as we shall see, Geoffrey of Monmouth. Henry, in any case, kept on trying to find new outlets. The sixth and final version – the only one which refers explicitly to the giving of a presentation copy – attempted an ambitious extension of the publishing circle. This time, the text of the *HA* was brought down to the coronation of Henry II, to December 1154, and a poem praising his virtues was added to its end.[126] After the poem, Henry of Huntingdon added the line 'Et iam regi novo nouus liber donandus est', indicating at least an intended presentation of a copy of the sixth version to the king himself. Not surprisingly, Henry again revised the portrait of King Henry I – the new king's grandfather – this time removing some of the vices he had added to the third version.[127] Like the fifth version, the sixth also became popular over time and, in some manuscripts, its text was used to provide the ending for an earlier version.[128] However, the manuscript evidence on early distribution is again scanty, with only one more or less complete copy from the twelfth century, datable to its second half, very likely after Henry of Huntingdon's own death.[129]

To sum up, the publishing history of the *HA* falls into two distinct phases. First, a long period of authorial hesitation and limited circulation, witnessed by the so-called first and second versions which, from Henry's perspective, were probably not 'versions' at all but just two copies of the draft at different stages. The start of the second phase is signalled by the so-called third version, made available in 1141/2. With this version, which could even be called the first 'edition' of the *HA*, we start to find clear traces of active authorial promotion of the text. Henry kept on revising and continuing the *HA* over a long period of time and he released it during that period again and again. The circle of people whom Henry sought to involve in the distribution of the finished versions is an impressive one:

---

[126] Henry of Huntingdon, *HA* x.40 (pp. 776–7).

[127] See Greenway, 'Introduction', pp. lxxvi–lxxvii.

[128] Cambridge, Corpus Christi College, MS 280, fols. 195r–209v (copied in s. xii²) and also as part of John of Worcester's chronicle, Cambridge, Corpus Christi College, MS 92, fols. 167v–175v (copied in s. xii²).

[129] Edinburgh, National Library of Scotland, MS Advocates' 33.5.2.

Alexander of Lincoln, Robert of Torigni, Robert de Chesney, and King Henry II.

In the long run, Henry's obstinacy in publishing paid off and the *HA* became widely available, remaining to the present day a standard authority for English history. However, while the overall count of copies datable to or antedating *c.*1200 is substantial (13), one also notes that no single version achieved great popularity quickly and that some of the versions appear to have remained available primarily in Lincoln and its environs. The only version that certainly circulated further immediately after its making was the fourth one, distributed via Robert of Torigni. Here – but probably only here – Henry's publishing circle was functioning effectively.

Indeed, perceived failure to achieve satisfactory dissemination may well have been one reason why so many different versions were launched in the first place. One explanation for the relatively limited early distribution could be that, so far as we know, Henry's text was not quickly available in any important insular monastic libraries, unlike William of Malmesbury's *Gesta regum* and *Gesta pontificum*, for instance. This may have been because Henry, as a secular clerk, did not have similarly natural connections to such centres, which were still at that point crucial textual supply points. The politically sensitive nature of his work might also have been an issue, ensuring that not only monastic but also aristocratic circles were wary of the *HA*.

4 Geoffrey of Monmouth

Geoffrey of Monmouth's (d. 1154/5) career was connected to the development of the schools of Oxford, where he was almost certainly a canon of St George's, a rich and short-lived college of secular canons located at the castle. Geoffrey is called *magister* in some of the documents he witnessed, which suggests that he had some involvement in teaching. Late in life he was elected bishop of St Asaph, a see he was, however, unable to enter because of the unstable political situation in northern Wales. During his years in Oxford, he composed three literary works, interlinked to one another, and it is to them that he owes his fame. First, there was the *Prophetia Merlini* (henceforth *PM*), a booklet released before late 1135, containing the Latin translation of a prophetic vision that Merlin had purportedly received in the sixth century. This was followed by *De gestis Britonum* (henceforth *DGB*), better known by its later title *Historia regum Britanniae*, another alleged translation of an old Brythonic text, which incorporated also the previously published *PM* (Book VII in *DGB*). Finally, in or soon after 1148, Geoffrey published a long hexameter epic, *Vita Merlini*, dedicated to the newly elected bishop of Lincoln, Robert de Chesney, his erstwhile colleague from St George's College.

DGB, by far the most popular of these works, survives in more than 220 medieval copies – more than five times as many as William's and Henry's histories.[130] Moreover, almost eighty of these copies can be dated to the twelfth century (including manuscripts dated to the turn of the century). There is little doubt that this contemporary popularity was in large measure due to the novelty and attraction of the work's content. *DGB* provided a previously unknown past for pre–Anglo-Saxon Britain, starting with the island's settlement by Trojan refugees. It also contained the first comprehensive narrative of King Arthur, who was at this time emerging as a popular figure of chivalrous literature. However, as I seek to demonstrate, Geoffrey was also exceptionally successful in creating a publishing circle that secured immediate distribution for his work.

The process leading to the publication of the complete *DGB* began with the release of a prelude, the *PM*, which was presented to Alexander of Lincoln sometime before late 1135, that is, well before the rest of *DGB* was finished.[131] According to Geoffrey's own testimony, the *PM* was sent to

---

[130] For the manuscripts, see Crick, *Summary Catalogue*, supplemented by her 'Two Newly Located Manuscripts of Geoffrey of Monmouth's *Historia regum Britanniae*', *Arthurian Literature*, 13 (1995), 151–6 and Tahkokallio, 'Update to the List of Manuscripts'. In 2015, another early fourteenth-century copy surfaced at auction (Christie's, London, Sale 1568) and was bought by Trinity College, Dublin.

[131] The date is based on the fact that Orderic Vitalis had access to the *PM* while Henry I (d. 1 December 1135) was still alive. See Orderic Vitalis, *Historia ecclesiastica*, ed. M. Chibnall, 6 vols. (Oxford: Clarendon Press, 1969–80), vol. 6, p. 381, xii.47 (iv.486). On the dating of the passage, see M. Chibnall, 'Introduction', in Orderic Vitalis, *Historia ecclesiastica*, vol. 6, ed. M. Chibnall

Alexander with a dedicatory letter.[132] Alexander spent much of 1134 and 1135 in Normandy.[133] We also know that Orderic Vitalis had read the *PM* in St Evroult (Normandy) well before December 1135 and that six out of nine twelfth-century copies of the independently published *PM* are continental.[134] It appears likely that Alexander was responsible for initiating the continental dissemination, in a manner that is similar to his role in the distribution of the fourth version of the *HA*. Either the *PM* was presented to

(Oxford: Clarendon Press, 1978), pp. xvii–xxvii, at p. xviii. See also N. Wright, 'Introduction', in *The 'Historia regum Britannie' of Geoffrey of Monmouth, vol. 1: Bern, Burgerbibliothek, MS. 568*, ed. N. Wright (Cambridge: D.S.Brewer, 1985), pp. ix–lix, at pp. xii–xvi, and Reeve, 'Introduction', p. viii.

[132] Geoffrey tells us about the separate publication, according to him at Alexander's instigation, in *DGB* §109 (pp. 142–3). The manuscripts of the separate *PM* sometimes include and sometimes omit this letter, which suggests it may have been a physically separate document – a practice which would find a parallel in the publishing history of William of Malmesbury's *GRA*.

[133] Alexander went to King Henry's court in Normandy at some point in 1134 (Henry of Huntingdon, *HA* vii.43, (p. 490)). In September 1134, he witnessed a royal charter at Verneuil (Johnson and Cronne (eds.), *Regesta Regum Anglo-Normannorum*, 1066–1154, vol. 2, no. 1895) and, probably around the same time, King Henry secured Lincoln's privileges, at Arganchy and Rouen, presumably at Alexander's initiative (*ibid.*, nos. 1899, 1911). Alexander was back in England by Easter 1136 when he witnessed King Stephen's charter in London (H. A. Cronne, H. W. C. Davis, and R. H. C. Davis (eds.), *Regesta Regum Anglo-Normannorum 1066–1154, vol. 3, Regesta Regis Stephani ac Mathildis Imperatricis ac Gaufridi et Henrici Ducum Normannorum 1135–1154* (Oxford: Clarendon Press, 1968), no. 46).

[134] The continental manuscripts are Berlin, Staatsbibliothek, MS theol. lat. qu. 328 (s. xii²); Paris, Bibliothèque nationale de France, MSS lat. 2935 (s. xii), lat. 6237 (s. xii²), lat. 6274 (s. xii^{med/2}), lat. 15172, and Città del Vaticano, Biblioteca Apostolica Vaticana, MS Reg. lat. 807 (s. xii²). The three insular copies with the independently published text (i.e. excluding texts extracted from the complete *DGB*) are Liège, Bibliothèques de l'Université de Liège, MS 369C (s. xii^{med}); Lincoln, Cathedral Library, MS 214 (s. xii^{med}), and Oxford, Lincoln College, MS Lat. 27 (s. xii).

him while he was in England, and he took it to Normandy with him, or Geoffrey somehow had it delivered to him across the Channel.

In Britain, too, the fact that two of the three twelfth-century copies have a connection to Lincoln may also be a reflection of Alexander's connections. One manuscript, of unknown origin and provenance, now belongs to Lincoln Cathedral Library (MS 214). The medieval provenance, and probably the origin, of the other is the Gilbertine house of Sempringham in Lincolnshire, Alexander's foundation.[135] A Durham origin has been suggested for the third insular manuscript, Liège 369 C, a connection not incompatible with a Lincoln origin.[136] While the *PM* apparently did not become a great bestseller on its own, the circumstantial evidence suggests that Alexander was involved in its early distribution. Notwithstanding, Geoffrey later complained that this dedication to Alexander had not been richly rewarded.[137] This sounds more like a complaint about a lack of career advancement than of literary success, reminding us of Felicity Riddy's point that what authors sought with patronage may not chiefly have been publicity and literary fame.[138]

Once Geoffrey had completed his main work, *DGB*, he in any case turned to a different dedicatee, one who had already demonstrated interest in William of Malmesbury's historical writing: Robert of Gloucester. While the dedicatory history of *DGB*, discussed further in what follows, has its famous complications, recent textual work has demonstrated beyond doubt that its first version was dedicated to Robert alone and he, consequently,

---

[135] Oxford, Lincoln College, MS Lat. 27, bears a Sempringham ex libris datable to *c.*1200 (fol. 6v) and contains two letters to St Gilbert of Sempringham.

[136] B. Meehan, 'Geoffrey of Monmouth, *Prophecies of Merlin*: New Manuscript Evidence', *Bulletin of the Board of Celtic Studies* 28 (1978), 37–46, at 43–4. See also C. Eckhardt, 'Geoffrey of Monmouth's *Prophetia Merlini* and the construction of Liège University MS 369C', *Manuscripta*, 32 (1988), 176–84.

[137] 'Ergo meis ceptis faveas vatemque tueri | auspicio meliore velis quam fecerit alter | cui modo succedis merito promotus honori'; Geoffrey of Monmouth, *Life of Merlin: Vita Merlini*, ed. B. Clarke (Cardiff: University of Wales Press, 1973), ll. 7–9 (pp. 52–3).

[138] Riddy, '"Publication" before Print', pp. 32–3.

must have received a presentation copy soon after work was finished.[139] The *terminus post quem non* for the public availability of *DGB* and, thus, for this presentation, is January 1139, when Robert of Torigni surprised Henry of Huntingdon with his copy of Geoffrey's work.[140] At the same time, the presentation probably did not occur very much before that date, since it is unlikely that Henry could have remained unaware of *DGB* for long, especially if it had entered into circulation in England.

Examining Robert of Gloucester's itinerary in this light makes it possible to define more closely the possible times and places for the original presentation of the work. Robert came from Normandy to England for King Stephen's Easter court of 1136 and returned to Normandy on Easter Sunday, 1137. His next visit to England was in September 1139.[141] This means that Robert was presented with *DGB* either in England between the Easters of 1136 and 1137 or in Normandy between Easter 1137 and the end of 1138 (to allow time for the making of Robert of Torigni's copy, finished by January 1139). Either way, the earliest evidence for its dissemination comes from the Continent and the textual history also indicates that it was there that the work first became generally available, via the presentation copy. If Geoffrey had given the book to Robert in England, it would probably have been only shortly before Easter 1137 and his departure.

Robert's role both in initiating the circulation of *DGB* on the Continent and, later, in contributing to its availability in Britain turns out to have been substantial. Much may be uncovered by fitting together evidence from the textual history and the manuscripts with available information about his movements and activities. The starting point is the observation that all early continental manuscripts descend from a single (now lost) exemplar, called

---

[139] Reeve, 'Introduction', pp. ix–x, xix. For the (much older) argument on the primacy of the dedication to Robert based on the content of the work, see Tatlock, *The Legendary History of Britain*, p. 436.

[140] As reported in *Letter to Warin*, Henry of Huntingdon, *HA*, pp. 558–9.

[141] For Robert's itinerary, see William of Malmesbury, *Historia Novella*, ed. E. King, trans. K. R. Potter (Oxford: Clarendon Press, 1998), §466 (pp. 21–2) and §478 (p. 34). See also Crouch, 'Robert, Earl of Gloucester, and the Daughter of Zelophehad', 232.

phi by Michael Reeve, editor of *DGB*.[142] Phi had the earliest of the three authorially released versions of the text that have been identified and it bore the dedication to Robert. Manuscripts descending from phi display a more structured division into books than members of other textual families and have more systematic rubrication. In other words, the layout of their exemplar was carefully executed. On this account, Reeve has suggested that phi was the presentation copy, as such a copy would have been likely to have received complete chapter markings, rubrics, and initials.[143] The fact that all the early continental copies of *DGB* descend from phi, without any interference from the other versions (whose influence is seen in the insular transmission from its beginning), and that they more faithfully than the early insular copies echo its division into eleven books, supports the idea that this dissemination originated with a single book – the presentation copy that Robert of Gloucester received from Geoffrey, either immediately before his arrival in Normandy (Easter 1137) or else once in Normandy (probably Caen), 1137–8.[144]

Certainly, the continental copying of *DGB* was initiated with great speed. Robert of Torigni had a copy, apparently a descendant of phi, in his possession by January 1139.[145] Furthermore, all continental descendants

---

[142] The divide between the homogeneous continental and heterogeneous insular textual situation is well evinced by the fact that, while Reeve's edition relies on twelve insular witnesses from the twelfth century, it uses only two continental twelfth-century manuscripts. The overall numbers of continental and insular twelfth-century manuscripts are similar.

[143] Reeve, 'Introduction', p. lx, and M. D. Reeve, 'The Transmission of the *Historia Regum Britanniae*', *The Journal of Medieval Latin*, 1 (1991), 73–117, at 102 n. 5.

[144] Delivery to Normandy is not an impossibility. Robert of Gloucester's main Norman residence was Caen Castle and the early Oxford colleges had links with the school in that city. See R. Foreville, 'L'École de Caen au XIe siècle et les origines normandes de l'université d'Oxford', in *Études médiévales offertes à M. Le Doyen Augustin Fliche de l'Institut* (Montpellier: Ch. Déhan, 1952), pp. 81–100.

[145] That Robert's text was a phi text approaches a logical necessity, given the textual picture of the transmission (i.e. the complete unavailability of other versions on the Continent until late in the twelfth century). The assumption is supported by

of phi descend through a curious bottleneck that came about during the very first steps of the continental transmission, probably because of accelerated copying. For the first half of the text (§§1–108), all early continental copies directly follow Paris, Bibliothèque Sainte-Geneviève, MS 2113 (henceforth, G). We know this for certain since they share unique transpositions that occurred during the copying of G. However, for the second half, they all (except one) descend directly from the exemplar of G.[146] This textual situation can only be explained by the existence of a manuscript copied partly from G and partly from its exemplar (which did not, of course, have the transpositions present in G), a copy we may call post-G, which then came to father the rest of the tradition. This break in the structure of post-G coincides with a section break in G itself. The first section, copied rather carefully by a single scribe, ends on the last folio of the fourth quire, six lines from the bottom of its verso. On this line, another scribe took over, continuing on the next quire and copying the rest of the work. The logical explanation for the structure of post-G would seem to be this: G was being copied from a copy of phi and, once the quires constituting the first half of G were finished, these quires were put to use as an exemplar for post-G, while the copying of the rest of the G was still going on using the original exemplar. Once §§1–108 of post-G had been copied from the first quires of G, G itself was completed and its exemplar became available and was used for the rest of post-G. This would have been an obvious choice, particularly since the second half of G is the result of visibly hurried scribal work, with many of the book divisions and initials indicating chapter division being omitted or sloppily executed.

The very first stages of copying appear to have been frantic. Not only were G and post-G produced with the emphasis on speed of production but

the fact that Henry of Huntingdon's *Letter to Warin* (i.e. an epitome of Robert's copy of *DGB*) very probably reflects a phi text, even though the matter cannot be verified with certainty because Henry recasts Geoffrey to a considerable extent; see Reeve, 'Introduction', p. xiii.

[146] See *ibid*. pp. xiv–xv. London, British Library, MS Add. 15732 (s. xii, continental) is the only twelfth-century manuscript descending directly from G in its entirety.

they had already been preceded by a copy of phi, a lost intermediary which served as their immediate exemplar.[147] Robert of Gloucester's involvement in this early continental copying is suggested by an important piece of textual evidence. Very soon after G and post-G had been copied, the continental transmission bifurcated. Two-thirds of the continental copies datable to the twelfth century descend directly from post-G but one-third (12 out of *c.*35), while in other respects completely similar, omit the name of the dedicatee in the dedicatory passage.[148] Neil Wright and Mary Garrison have suggested that the omission came about in a manuscript in which the place for the name of the dedicatee was left blank for later completion in another colour.[149] This was sometimes done: Robert of Gloucester's half-sister, Empress Matilda, owned a copy of Ekkehard of Aura's chronicle in which her name was inscribed in gold letters, obviously done at a stage in the manufacturing process later than the transcription of the text.[150] While most 'nameless-dedication' copies do not directly point out any omission in the exemplar but rather try to amend the situation, one of them does draw attention to an incomplete exemplar. This is Paris, Bibliothèque nationale de France, MS lat. 12943, a manuscript whose making can be localised to

---

[147] See Reeve, 'Introduction', pp. xiv–xv and Reeve, 'Transmission', pp. 85–87. The exemplar of G was later copied only in Britain. It may have been produced within Robert's household and travelled back to Britain with his court in September 1139.

[148] Aberystwyth, National Library of Wales, MS 11611 (s. xii$^{med/2}$); Auxerre, Bibliothèque municipale, MS 91 (s. xii/xiii); Brussels, Bibliothèque royale, MS 9871–9974 (s. xii/xiii); Cambridge, UL, MS Mm. 1. 34. (s. xii/xiii); Madrid, Biblioteca Nacional de España; MS 6319 (s. xii^2); Montpellier, Bibliothèque interuniversitaire, MS 92 (s. xii$^{3/4}$); Paris, BnF, MSS lat. 5233 (s. xii$^{2/ex}$), lat. 6041B (s. xii^2), lat. 6231, lat. 8501A (s. xii^2), lat. 18271 (s. xii^2), and Troyes, Médiathèque du Grand Troyes, MS 273bis (s. xii/xiii).

[149] See Reeve, 'Transmission', p. 81 n. 19 and J. Crick, *Historia Regum Britannie of Geoffrey of Monmouth IV: Dissemination and Reception in the Later Middle Ages* (Cambridge: D.S.Brewer, 1991), p. 118 n. 38. As both explain, the full argument, first made by Wright and developed by Garrison, has never been completely presented in print.

[150] Cambridge, Corpus Christi College, MS 373, fol. 95v.

Paris and dated to the late 1160s.[151] In this book, no attempt has been taken to smooth out the sentence made unintelligible by the missing words of the dedication. Instead, where the dedication ought to be, we read only 'deest' ('is missing'). In other words, the copyist noted the absence of the dedication in the exemplar, probably because there was an empty space.[152]

If, as seems likely, the nameless dedication went back to an unfinished luxury manuscript (the nameless master copy), its most probable *destinataire* would have been Robert of Gloucester himself. The changing of the single line which is missing would not have offered sufficient means to rededicate the work to another, since the dedicatory passage is much longer and contains, for example, a reference in another sentence to Robert's status as son of Henry I. It is furthermore very likely that the nameless master copy was one of the very first copies made on the Continent, since it is difficult to explain how a manuscript with such a glaring shortcoming at the very beginning of the text would come to have been used so extensively as an exemplar if the text had already been widely available. The probable use of the nameless master copy as an exemplar for a book made in Paris in the late 1160s hints at its presence there at that time, an interpretation supported by what we know about the medieval origins and provenances of other

---

[151] The manuscript contains accounts of judicial proceedings involving the abbey of Saint-Germain-des-Prés, datable to 1168 × 1169; see R. Poupardin (ed.), *Recueil des chartes de Saint-Germain-des-Prés*, vol. 1 (Paris: Champion, 1909), 147 (p. 217). These were copied immediately after *DGB*, by order of Abbot Hugh (1162–82), as is stated in the manuscript. Note that the pen flourishes seen in the initials of *DGB* display the so-called pointing-finger motif, first documented in Paris at this time. Indeed, its earliest dated occurrence is in a document concerning an affair in which the same Abbot Hugh was involved, from 1162 to 1163; P. Stirnemann, 'Fils de la vierge: L'initiale à filigranes parisiennes: 1140–1314', *Revue de l'Art*, 90 (1990), 58–73, at 61, 72.

[152] Furthermore, uniquely among the twelfth-century copies of *DGB*, the rubric of this manuscript refers to Geoffrey as a *magister* ('Incipit prefacio magistri Gaufridi Monemutensis in historia Britonum'). Geoffrey is given the title of magister in a number of documents in which he testifies. It appears likely that this rubric derives from the exemplar of Paris lat. 12943, i.e. possibly the nameless master copy.

members of the nameless-dedication family. These manuscripts, in as much as they can be localised, hail from the regions of Paris, Burgundy, Champagne, and Anjou, whereas the direct descendants of post-G cluster in Normandy, Flanders, and Picardy. Could it have been that the nameless master copy, once its text had been transcribed from post-G in Normandy, travelled south, perhaps to Paris, to receive fashionable illumination at the hands of the best artists of the time? On the Continent, the availability of bookmaking expertise was at any rate greater than in Geoffrey's Oxford ambit, where the original presentation copy had probably been produced.

According to Gaimar's *Estoire des Engleis*, Robert loaned a copy of *DGB* to Walter Espec, a Yorkshire magnate. This took place soon after his return to England in September 1139 (early 1140s at the latest).[153] Textual history and codicological evidence support this testimony and indicate that the book loan had a real effect on the distribution. Essentially, the influence of Robert's presentation copy is visible as an anomaly in the work's textual landscape in Britain. The great majority of the early British copies of *DGB* belong to a different branch of transmission than do the early continental phi manuscripts. They descend from so-called delta, which was apparently produced from Geoffrey's draft (of which phi was an earlier fair copy) after a series of authorial revisions. However, the predominantly continental phi tradition has a group of relatives in England, some of which are particularly important witnesses to the phi text and were used by Reeve in its editorial reconstruction.

---

[153] 'Robert li quens de Gloücestre | fist translater icele geste | solum les livres as Waleis | k'il aveient des bretons reis. | Walter Espec la demandat, | li quens Robert li enveiat . . .'; Geffrei Gaimar, *Estoire des Engleis*, ed. I. Short (Oxford: Oxford University Press, 2009), ll. 6449–54 (pp. 348–9). The precise date of Gaimar's *Estoire* remains open. Ian Short ('Gaimar's Epilogue and Geoffrey of Monmouth's Liber Vetustissimus', *Speculum*, 69 (1994), 323–43) has argued for an early date, in the 1130s, while Paul Dalton ('The Date of Geoffrey Gaimar's Estoire des Engleis, the Connections of his Patrons, and the Politics of Stephen's Reign', *The Chaucer Review*, 42 (2007), 23–47) has provided thorough and largely convincing criticism of Short's position. If we put together Short's and Dalton's arguments, both of which have their merits, 1141 transpires as the moment for which no central piece of evidence contradicts another.

The first group clusters around the twelfth-century manuscript Cambridge, Gonville & Caius College, MS 406/627, called Y by the editor. Y was kept, by *c.*1300, at Bridlington priory (OSA, Yorks ER), which belonged to a Yorkshire network of Augustinian houses in which Walter Espec took an interest.[154] Its twelfth-century marginalia suggests that the manuscript was already in Yorkshire by then.[155] The manuscript, furthermore, has unique and uniquely representational decoration. The initial B on the first page of the book (beginning the second chapter of *DGB*) contains two portraits, one in each lobe of the letter. The upper one is a figure with crown-like headgear. The one below is a grumpy-looking clerk. The images are not of the highest artistic standard and their iconography is by no means clear. In fact, the figure above, with flowing hair, might well be female. Yet one wonders whether these images, found directly below the dedicatory passage, in fact depict the author and the patron and derive from the decoration of the exemplar of Y.

Altogether nine British manuscripts are related to Y, six of these datable to the twelfth century.[156] Most of these have no early provenance but the manuscript textually closest to Y, Oxford, Bodleian Library, MS Fairfax 28, was in Nun Appleton, just outside of York, in the seventeenth century, as one part of the small and locally sourced Fairfax family collection.[157] This

---

[154] Walter was the patron of one member of this closely knit network, Kirkham priory, founded by 1130. See Burton, *Monastic Order in Yorkshire*, pp. 79–80 and Knowles, *Monastic Order*, p. 229.

[155] On the provenance, see Crick, *Summary Catalogue*, p. 50 and the marginalia in the manuscript (fol. 43r). The hand of the marginalia seems early, using, for instance, *e-caudata*.

[156] Aberystwyth, National Library of Wales, MSS Peniarth 42 (s. xii$^{2/ex}$), Porkington 17 (s. xiii$^{med/2}$); Cambridge, Gonville & Caius College, MS 103/55 (s. xii^{ex}), London, British Library, MS Harley 225 (s. xii$^{2/ex}$); London, Lambeth Palace Library, MS 188 (s. xiv), 454, fols. 124r–204r (s. xii$^{med/ex}$); Oxford, Bodleian Library, MSS Fairfax 28 (s. xii$^{med/2}$), Rawlinson B. 148 (s. xiii^{med}), and Philadelphia, The Free Library, MS E.247 (s. xii^{ex}).

[157] For the manuscripts, see F. Madan, H. H. E. Craster, and N. Denholm-Young, *A Summary Catalogue of Western Manuscripts in the Bodleian Library at Oxford*, vol. 2, part 2 (Oxford: Clarendon Press, 1937), pp. 772–89.

manuscript has an opening rubric reading 'Domino Rodberto Comiti'. A similar address to Robert, similar in diplomatic form to epistolary address clauses, is included in the rubrics of some of the continental descendants of phi as well, including G and post-G. It is not found in other branches of the textual tradition and the logical assumption is that it reflects the rubrication of the presentation copy.[158] Moreover, a member of the Y group was used by Alfred of Beverley in Yorkshire, *c.*1143, as he created his epitome of *DGB*.[159] We know that Walter's copy of *DGB* was kept at Helmsley Castle, twenty-four miles north of York, and it appears highly likely that these manuscripts descend from it. Apparently, the introduction of the text to Yorkshire by Robert's and Walter's cooperation provided a significant boost to its distribution.

We have already encountered the other important insular witness to the mainly continental phi tradition: London, British Library, MS Royal 13 D. II, which was, by the thirteenth century (at the latest), at Margam Abbey (OCist, Glam), one of Robert of Gloucester's few monastic foundations. This manuscript contains excellent textual witnesses of William of Malmesbury's *GRA*, the 'Robertian recension' of his *Historia novella*, and *DGB*.[160] According to Reeve, the Margam manuscript is textually the best representative of the phi family of *DGB* – and also, arguably, the best witness to the text of *DGB* overall. In Michael Reeve's words, 'a transcript of M [= Margam Abbey MS] would be a tolerable substitute for an edition'.[161] Given the ensemble of texts and their quality and the early

---

[158] See Crick, *Dissemination and Reception*, p. 125. A potential exception is a fifteenth-century manuscript now in Cambridge (UL, Dd. 6. 7) but its rubric could also descend from the Leiden group. It was copied at St Albans Abbey, apparently using a large number of different textual sources; see Crick, *Dissemination and Reception*, p. 131 and Reeve, 'Introduction', p. xxxvi.

[159] Alfred of Beverley, *Annales*, ed. T. Hearne (Oxford: E Theatro Sheldoniano, 1716). See also Reeve, 'Introduction', p. xiv.

[160] On the 'Robertian' nature of the text of *Historia novella*, see King, 'Introduction', pp. lxxvii–xciv. On the possible connection to Roger of Worcester in particular, see *ibid.* pp. xci–xciv.

[161] Reeve, 'Introduction', p. xvi.

home of this manuscript, it is difficult to escape the conclusion that the exemplar used in the copying of *DGB* was the original presentation copy given to Robert in 1137 or 1138.

By all accounts, Robert of Gloucester was the key figure in Geoffrey's publishing circle. He certainly contributed significantly to the rapid dissemination of the text which bore his name as dedicatee and in fact his role may have been even more far-reaching. *DGB* is also found with two double dedications, both objects of much previous debate. The first, and by far the more common in the manuscripts, dedicates the work jointly to Robert and Waleran, count of Meulan. Robert and Waleran were not friends or allies. During the reign of Henry I, Waleran, who had been brought up at the royal court, had plotted against the king, Robert's father and protector, and been imprisoned for five years. Stephen's seizure of the crown opened new avenues for Waleran's ambition. He quickly became the new king's trusted counsellor and had great power vested in his hands. This put him in direct conflict with Robert of Gloucester, whose commitment to Stephen was never anything but superficial and who eventually challenged Stephen's right to the crown, backing his sister Matilda's claim.

It used to be argued that the double dedication to Robert and Waleran was the original one and that a book (or, more likely, books) bearing it had been presented to the magnates at King Stephen's Easter Court of 1136. This presentation, so it was thought, carried a plea to the two rivals to maintain peace. Such a chronology, once obstinately championed by the discoverer of the double dedication, Acton Griscom, and echoed by some relatively recent scholarship as well,[162] has been made untenable by the

---

[162] A. Griscom, 'The Date of Composition of Geoffrey of Monmouth's *Historia*: New Manuscript Evidence', *Speculum*, 1 (1926), 129–56 and *The Historia Regum Britanniae of Geoffrey of Monmouth* (London: Longmans, Green, 1929), pp. 42–98; Dumville, 'An Early Text of Geoffrey of Monmouth's *Historia Regum Britanniae*', 27; Crouch, 'Robert, Earl of Gloucester, and the Daughter of Zelophehad', 230; Short, 'Gaimar's Epilogue and Geoffrey of Monmouth's Liber Vetustissimus', 338–9, and M. Aurell, *La légende du Roi Arthur: 550–1250* (Paris: Perrin, 2007), p. 102.

recent uncovering of the textual history of the work.[163] It is now clear that the double dedication post-dated the dedication to Robert alone and this makes its suggested early date unlikely in the extreme. Publication of *DGB* before Robert and Waleran's falling-out would require that two versions – one dedicated to Robert alone and another dedicated to Robert and Waleran – were put into circulation in England in 1136 and such widely publicised early availability is impossible to reconcile with the fact that Henry of Huntingdon was unaware of the work until January 1139.[164]

A much more plausible date for the creation of the double dedication is provided by the circumstances in which Robert and Waleran made their peace. King Stephen's defeat and capture at the Battle of Lincoln, February 1141, made his position utterly hopeless. In the following summer, Waleran abandoned Stephen's cause and was reconciled with Robert and Matilda after two years of open and destructive warfare. At this point, the two counts met, witnessing charters by which Bordesley Abbey passed from Waleran to Matilda, as part of the peace-making process.[165] The Bordesley charters were written at Devizes but, throughout the summer of 1141, Matilda's court lodged at Oxford, Geoffrey of Monmouth's probable place

---

[163] At *DGB* §177.1 Geoffrey refers to his dedicatee in the singular as 'consul auguste', the use of 'consul' as a title being compatible with Robert's position. This suggests that the recipient of the work had already been decided when the last book was begun. For the crucial textual evidence on the primacy of the dedication to Robert, see Reeve, 'Introduction', pp. ix–x and xix.

[164] Henry's testimony of itself has led several scholars to reason that the most likely moment for the act of publishing was shortly before his discovery of the text, probably in 1138. See Tatlock, *Legendary History of Britain*, pp. 433–4; Wright, 'Introduction', pp. xv–xvi, and J. Gillingham, 'The Context and Purposes of Geoffrey of Monmouth's *History of the Kings of Britain*', in J. Gillingham, *English in the Twelfth Century* (Woodbridge: Boydell Press, 2000), pp. 19–39, at p. 20.

[165] Cronne, Davis, and Davis (eds.), *Regesta Regum Anglo-Normannorum*, 1066–1154, vol. 3, nos. 115, 116, dated to 25 July–15 September but in fact predating 12 August; see D. Crouch, *The Reign of King Stephen, 1135–1154* (Harlow: Longman, 2000), pp. 183–4 n. 41; and Chibnall, *Empress Matilda*, pp. 134–5. For the context of the charters, see *ibid.*, pp. 100–2 and Crouch, *Reign of King Stephen*, pp. 171–83.

of residence. I suggest that this was the context for the making of the first joint dedication and that it was produced with Robert's participation.

Such a possibility had actually been considered by Acton Griscom and his rejection of the idea buried this obvious solution to the dedicatory puzzle for decades.[166] Griscom's thinking was, however, conditioned by the incorrect assumption that the joint dedication would have been the first and original one. He also made questionable interpretations about its making and purpose. First, Griscom supposed that the making of such a double dedication, placing Robert and Waleran on an equal footing, would have been Geoffrey's decision alone. But would Geoffrey not have needed to take into account Robert's reaction to the joint presentation of the work to a new patron with whom Robert had a particularly fraught relationship? Second, Griscom assumed that the wording of the double dedication would have necessitated a thorough and sincere reconciliation between the two magnates, primarily because it addressed Waleran as 'the other pillar of our kingdom' (*altera regni nostri columna*).[167] But does a courtesy of this sort warrant conclusions about what Robert and Waleran really thought of one another? If we suspect that Robert may not have felt very warmly towards Waleran, who had ravaged his lands and with whom he shared a long history of mistrust extending back into the reign of Henry I, the text of the double dedication leaves plenty of room for ironic interpretations as well. The dedication lauds Waleran's courage: 'you surpassed your comrades in boldness, and you learned, like your father before you, to become a terror to your enemies and to be a protector of your own.'[168] But they probably both remembered that, in the Battle of Lincoln, Robert's triumph, which had brought the pair to the negotiation table, Waleran had conspicuously fled the battlefield on

---

[166] Griscom, *Historia Regum Britanniae of Geoffrey of Monmouth*, pp. 69–70.

[167] Geoffrey of Monmouth, *DGB* §4 (pp. 4–5).

[168] '. . . commilitones tuos audacter supergressus et terror hostium existere et protectio tuorum esse paternis auspiciis addidicisti'; Geoffrey of Monmouth, *DGB* §3 (p. 5, note to line 23).

horseback while his lord, King Stephen, whom he had vowed to protect and who had engaged in the battle on foot, kept on fighting until captured.[169]

However we interpret its message, the dedicatory text makes it clear that a copy of the work was given to Waleran, since Geoffrey asked him to take under his protection both himself and 'the book given out for your delight' (*codicemque ad oblectamentum tui editum*).[170] Whether Waleran contributed much to the further circulation of the work is another matter. He travelled to Normandy soon after the summer of 1141 but, on the Continent, the double dedication is found only in two manuscripts. Both these manuscripts, furthermore, represent textually the continental mainstream of the transmission – the text descending from phi presented to Robert alone – with the dedication to Waleran simply added from another textual source.

In England, at the same time, a total of eight copies survive bearing the joint dedication from the twelfth century – not an insignificant number.[171] All

---

[169] Henry of Huntingdon, *HA* x.18 (pp. 736–7). In the pre-battle speech that Henry of Huntingdon put into the mouth of Robert of Gloucester, Robert accused Waleran of being 'expert in deceit, a master of trickery, who was born with wickedness in his blood, falsehood in his mouth, sloth in his deeds, a braggart by nature, stout-hearted in talk, faint-hearted in deed, the last to muster, the first to decamp, slow to attack, quick to retreat' (' doli callidus, fallendi artifex, cui innata est in corde nequitia, in ore fallatia, in opere pigricia, gloriosus corde, magnanimus ore, pusillanimis opere, ad congrediendum ultimus, ad digrediendum primus, tardus ad pugnam, uelox ad fugam'); Henry of Huntingdon, *HA* x.15 (pp. 728–9). These words may or may not reflect Robert's real thoughts but they support the idea that Waleran's knightly reputation had been called into question by some of his contemporaries.

[170] Geoffrey of Monmouth, *DGB* §4 (pp. 4–5).

[171] Cambridge, Trinity College, MS O. 2. 21 (s. xiii/xiv); Cambridge, University Library, MSS Ii. 1. 14 (s. xii), Ii 4. 4 (s. xii^{ex}); London, British Library, MS Lansdowne 732 (s. xii/xiii); New Haven (CT), Yale University Library, MS 590 (s. xii); Oxford, Bodleian Library, MSS Add. A.61 (s. xiii), Bodley 514 (s. xii^2); Paris, Bibliothèque nationale de France, MS lat. 6040 (s. xii^{med}); Città del Vaticano, Biblioteca Apostolica Vaticana, MSS Reg. lat. 692 (s. xii; joint dedication added in the margin but later erased) and Vat. lat. 2005 (s. xii;

of these copies descend from a single manuscript, Paris BnF, MS lat. 6040, of English origin. We can be sure of their dependence on this particular book since one of its quires was copied from a different textual source than the rest, by a different scribe. This combination of textual traditions, resulting from contemporary repair of physical damage that took place as the manuscript was being bound, is repeated in all the manuscripts with the double dedication (except the continental manuscripts which conflate it with a phi text).[172] The main source of Paris 6040 was delta, the authorial version post-dating phi from which most of the early British copies descend. However, the odd quire follows phi, i.e. the presentation copy given to Robert. Intriguingly, the phi part of Paris 6040 descends from phi through a similar intermediary copy as the Yorkshire group, the probable result of Robert's book loan to Walter Espec. Paris 6040 is an important textual witness to both phi and delta and was used by Reeve in establishing the text of *DGB* for both these textual families. It is thus textually close to manuscripts that we can associate with Geoffrey *and* with Robert and, in all likelihood, it stems from the context in which the presentation copy to Waleran was originally produced, although its poor quality makes it unlikely to have been the presentation copy itself. Whereas Waleran's role in the distribution must have been limited, the involvement of Robert in the creation of the joint dedication would fit logically with his attested active role in the circulation of *DGB*.

Circumstantial evidence, furthermore, points to the possibility that the other joint dedication, to Robert and to King Stephen, was also launched with Robert's (or Matilda's) participation. This famous dedication is found in a single manuscript, Bern, Burgerbibliothek, MS 569, datable to the second half of the twelfth century. It was executed with minimal effort, by changing thirteen words in the earlier joint dedication so that King

---

bears the double dedication but follows the text that typically accompanies it only for the first chapters).

[172] The top-left corner of the book was completely cut off and then immediately repaired. A contemporary hand – very probably that of the original scribe – supplied the text that had gone missing on patches of parchment glued to every bifolium. It was presumably during this extensive repair that one quire went missing and was recopied from another source.

Stephen was put in Robert's place as the first dedicatee and Robert was moved over to occupy Waleran's position. Given the lazy nature of this reworking and the textual corruption of the manuscript in which it is found, it is not possible to account straightforwardly for the origin of this dedication and it has been suggested that someone other than Geoffrey may have written it.[173] But it is difficult to imagine a person entirely disconnected from the author imposing such modifications to a copy so as to present it to the king. In what sense could this kind of faked dedication – for it is always Geoffrey who appears as the composer in the prologue – have pleased Stephen, especially since the text was already in circulation with a dedication to his bitter enemy?

The more likely alternative seems, again, joint agency on the part of the author and the original dedicatee(s). A probable context for the giving of the book to Stephen emerges from the curious circumstances of September to October 1141. Robert had by then also been taken prisoner and the negotiations for exchanging him with Stephen (who remained in Matilda's custody) were taking place. We know that the text was fashionable at this time. Writing very soon after, in 1143, Alfred of Beverley stated that 'it was a sign of rusticity' not to be familiar with the stories told in *DGB* and, indeed, that he had often blushed in conversations because of his ignorance of the work.[174] Robert and Matilda could well have played for diplomatic effect on Robert's role as the primary dedicatee of such an uncommonly sought-after work. It would not have hurt them, either, that the text also

---

[173] See, in particular, E. Brugger, 'Zu Galfrid von Monmouth's Historia Regum Britanniae', *Zeitschrift für französische Sprache und Literatur*, 57 (1933), 257–332, at 272–6. See also Reeve, 'Transmission', p. 76 and *Geoffrey of Monmouth*, p. xix.

[174] 'Ferebantur tunc temporis per ora multorum narraciones de hystoria Britonum, notamque rusticitatis incurrebat, qui talium narracionum scienciam non habebabt. Fateor tamen propter antiquitatis reverenciam, quae mihi semper veneracioni fuerat, tamen propter narrandi urbanitatem, quae mihi minime, junioribus vero memoriter & jocunde tunc aderat, inter tales confabulatores saepe erubescebam, quod paefatam hystoriam necdum attigeram. Quid plura? Quaesivi historiam, et ea vix inventa, leccioni ejus intentissime studium adhibui'; Alfred of Beverley, *Annales*, p. 2.

argued the case for the viability of female rulership in showing several capable historical queens who had governed Britain or that it portrayed Robert's crucial allies, the Welsh, in a more positive light than was typical for the Anglo-Norman literary imagination.[175]

As with the copy presented to Waleran, the book given to King Stephen had very little impact on the further dissemination of *DGB*. The only manuscript to contain the dedication was copied in Fécamp, probably in the last quarter of the twelfth century.[176] In this manuscript, *DGB* is followed by Aelred of Rievaulx's *Vita Sancti Edwardi*, composed sometime between 1161 and 1163 and dedicated to Henry II. The exemplar used for this text was of English origin. In the absence of earlier continental witnesses, one suspects that the same was true of the exemplar that the Fécamp scribes used for *DGB*.[177] Given Robert's active role in the distribution, and the probably widely known association of the text with him, it is not surprising that we see much less trace of the secondary dedicatees promoting the dissemination of *DGB*.

While Robert was undoubtedly a key person within Geoffrey's publishing circle, he was not the sole distribution channel for the text. Evidently, institutional collections were important for the transmission of *DGB* as well. We know that Robert of Torigni had a copy by January 1139 and that, *c*.1150, he arranged for the production of a compilation containing it for the library of the abbey of Le Bec.[178] Over the course of the twelfth century, copies of *DGB* stemming from the Le Bec book or its exemplar (Robert of Torigni's copy?) were produced at least for the libraries of Anchin

---

[175] For Geoffrey's advocacy of female rulership, see F. Tolhurst, *Geoffrey of Monmouth and the Translation of Female Kingship* (Basingstoke: Palgrave Macmillan, 2013). For the deteriorating contemporary image of the Celtic peoples, see J. Gillingham, 'The Beginnings of English Imperialism', *Journal of Historical Sociology*, 5 (1992), 392–409.

[176] Bern, Burgerbibliothek, MS 568.

[177] For the structure of the Bern manuscript, see Wright, 'Introduction', pp. xxxv–xliii.

[178] Leiden, Universiteitsbibliotheek, MS BPL 20.

(Flanders),[179] Marchiennes (Flanders),[180] Chaalis (Picardy),[181] and Jumièges (Normandy).[182] In Britain, there is less firm evidence for the ownership of copies of *DGB* by institutional libraries in the twelfth century. However, a list of books copied for Glastonbury Abbey at the instigation of Henry of Blois (abbot, 1126–71) includes Geoffrey's work, showing that, at an early date, *DGB* had entered the Glastonbury collection, which had been a significant factor in the success of the *GRA*.[183] While these are clear instances of transmission relying on monastic networks, both the Le Bec and the Glastonbury cases also make it evident that the copying happened at the initiative of an individual bibliophile. It is highly likely that other similarly scholarly monks, invisible to us now, were of equal significance in the general monastic transmission.

In Britain, besides aristocratic and monastic circles, the text was also available directly from the producer. As has been said, not all manuscripts descended from the presentation copy given to Robert of Gloucester. Geoffrey kept on revising the text and produced the so-called sigma and delta versions of the text (sigma covering only §§118–208). Delta was probably the main source for the book made for Waleran but this version additionally circulated with the dedication to Robert. Four of the delta manuscripts, all British ones, are considered by Reeve to have independent textual authority and thus descend from Geoffrey's delta autograph by independent routes.[184] All of these manuscripts are early ones, datable to

---

[179] Douai, Bibliothèque municipale, MS 880 (s. xii²). See Crick, *Summary Catalogue*, pp. 93–4.

[180] Douai, Bibliothèque municipale, MS 882 (s. xii^ex). See Crick, *Summary Catalogue*, pp. 94–8.

[181] Paris, BnF, MS lat. 17569 (s. xii/xiii). See Crick, *Summary Catalogue*, pp. 292–3.

[182] Rouen, Bibliothèque municipale, MS U.74 (s. xii/xiii). See Crick, *Summary Catalogue*, pp. 305–6.

[183] For the list, see Sharpe, *English Benedictine Libraries*, pp. 160–5 (*DGB* appears as item B37. 21, p. 163). The list is preserved in Cambridge, Trinity College, MS R. 5. 33 (s. xiii^med), fol. 23r.

[184] Cambridge, Corpus Christi College, MS 281 (s. xii²); Cambridge, University Library, MS Dd. 6. 12 (s. xii^med); Oxford, Bodleian Library, MS Rawlinson C. 152 (s. xii^med/2), and Salisbury, Cathedral Library, MS 121 (s. xii^med/2).

around the middle of the twelfth century or soon after, and they suggest frequent early copying of Geoffrey's own working manuscript.[185]

One of these delta manuscripts, furthermore, conveys distinguishable signs of further authorial revision. This is Oxford, Bodleian Library, MS Rawlinson C. 152, from the middle of the twelfth century, having a peculiar tall and narrow format (300 × 165 mm).[186] In this manuscript, the prologue to the *PM* is idiosyncratic. Whereas manuscripts regularly include the full dedicatory letter to Alexander of Lincoln, in this copy the letter is replaced by a newly formulated, apparently autobiographical passage to the same effect, in which Geoffrey refers to himself as *pudibundus brito* ('bashful Briton').[187] Furthermore, the text of *DGB* has a unique and curious opening rubric, 'Gaufridi Monemutensis de gestis Britonum secundum Caratonum Editio'.[188] It has been plausibly argued that the work of Caratonus, given here as Geoffrey's source, should be equated with the book that Geoffrey mentions as his source in the prologue and the epilogue – the very old book in the Welsh language, which he had from Walter, archdeacon of Oxford.[189]

Besides the textual history, one contemporary reference hints at the distribution of exemplars directly from Oxford, something which can perhaps be associated with the version of the text presented by Rawlinson C. 152. In his epilogue to the *Estoire des Engleis*, Gaimar mentions not only the book that Walter Espec was given by Robert of Gloucester but also

---

[185] CCCC 281 was possibly made at the Cluniac priory of St Andrew, Northampton; see Crick, *Summary Catalogue*, pp. 35–7.

[186] One scribe had the main responsibility for the work but he or she was helped by others in the second quire and towards the end of the book, where both the varying quality of handwriting and abridgement of the text indicate haste in getting the work finished. According to Reeve, the copy 'omits a large number of dispensable phrases' from *DGB* §173 onwards; Reeve, 'Transmission', p. 80.

[187] See *ibid.*, pp. 79–80.

[188] This rubric is in the same red ink which was used for the initials and, judging by their style, both the initials and the rubric appear to be contemporary with the text.

[189] Geoffrey of Monmouth, *DGB* §1 (pp. 4–5) and §208 (pp. 280–1), and Reeve, 'Transmission', 80.

another book of Welsh history, which he had 'purchasé – u fust a dreit u fust a tort – le bon livere de Oxeford, ki fust Walter l'arcediaen'. This book, Gaimar writes, he used as a supplementary source as he was himself penning a copy of the book he had received from Walter.[190] It seems highly unlikely that Gaimar would have had access to Geoffrey's purported Welsh source, which very likely did not exist and which Gaimar even more likely would not have been able to read had it existed at all. This reference in effect suggests that Gaimar had in fact two copies of the *De gestis* at his disposal, one that he had procured from Oxford and another that came via Walter Espec. The Oxford copy may have been related to Rawlinson C. 152, with its rubric referring to Caratonus, i.e. the purported source. The origin of C. 152 is unclear and it has no early surviving descendants. However, while two thirteenth-century copies descending from it were made at St Albans,[191] the most numerous of its late medieval descendants have associations with the north of England, i.e. in the landscape familiar to Gaimar and Walter Espec.[192]

One cannot but conclude that Geoffrey played the game of publishing deliberately and successfully. He succeeded in creating an effective publishing circle, making use of aristocratic, monastic, and learned networks of the time. The narrative sources combined with information from textual history and manuscripts suggest that individuals with high status and resources, like Robert of Gloucester and Henry of Blois, or with special influence over the transmission of texts, like Robert of Torigni, advertised the work, commissioned new copies, and provided exemplars for others

---

[190] Geffrei Gaimar, *Estoire des Engleis*, ll. 6443–60.

[191] See Reeve, 'Transmission', p. 116. The manuscripts are Cambridge, University Library, MS Dd. 6. 7 + Oxford, Bodleian Library, MS Bodley 585 (s. xv) and London, BL, MS Royal 13 D. V (s. xiii$^{1/2}$). On their provenance, see Crick, *Summary Catalogue*, pp. 72, 184–6.

[192] The manuscript (s. xiv$^{1/2}$) consisting of London, British Library, MS Cotton Titus A. XVIII + Cotton Vespasian B. X + Cotton Fragments XXIX (fols. 36–9) was in Durham in the Middle Ages, as was Oxford, Bodleian Library, MS Laud Misc. 720 (s. xiii^2). Oxford, Bodleian Library, MS Jones 48 (s. xiv) has a fifteenth-century Furness (Lancs) provenance and Oxford All Souls' College, MS 35 (xiii$^{1/2}$) was in the possession of a Scottish scholar in the thirteenth century.

seeking access to the text. Very probably, Robert was also involved in arranging new publishing events, such as presentations of tinkered copies to Waleran and King Stephen. That Geoffrey's work ultimately became so much more popular than Henry of Huntingdon's and William of Malmesbury's must have owed a great deal to its novel and attractive content; but one cannot fail to notice that his publishing circle also left us with many more direct and indirect traces of its activity. Geoffrey's success was won over within his own lifetime, as is evinced both by the large numbers of surviving early copies and by contemporary accounts. In his *Vita Merlini* (*c*.1148) Geoffrey stated that *DGB* was *celebrata per orbem*,[193] and, despite the self-congratulatory tone, he provides here, for once, an accurate historical testimony.

5 Conclusions

The processes by which William of Malmesbury, Henry of Huntingdon, and Geoffrey of Monmouth made their works available to their audiences unite the two main components of our definition of publishing – the releasing of intellectual content and the making of its materiality publicly available. For these authors, publishing involved releasing, and sometimes rereleasing, texts, as well as building a circle of patrons and bibliophiles to advance their distribution. This should obviously not lead us to think that successful publishing in a manuscript context would always need to be in equal parts authorial and promotional. In reaching an audience, many twelfth-century authors, such as Hugh and Richard of the abbey of Saint-Victor in Paris or Alexander Nequam, prior of Cirencester Abbey, continued to depend on a community that would promote their work and help in producing copies of it. It is also true that achieving bestseller status depended in significant measure on factors inherent to the literary product. In our case, the fact that William, Henry, and Geoffrey are still among the most widely read of medieval historians is indeed a lasting testimony to their skill as writers. Furthermore, William and Henry wrote the first real histories of England since Bede, and Geoffrey's history, largely of his own

---

[193] Geoffrey of Monmouth, *Vita Merlini*, ll. 1529 (pp. 123–5).

invention, covered an even greater patch of uncharted territory. There was, in other words, a demand for the content they produced.

Nevertheless, the speed at which all these works managed to enter wide circulation, taken together with the quantity of publishing activity that can be documented across the authors' lifetimes, would indicate that the role of authorial effort in these cases was significant. To contextualise the matter of publishing and the success of our three authors further, it is useful to take a brief look at other writers active in the same genre and in the same period. Such a comparative exercise reminds us, first, that many historical works were published in a very small way, with hardly any authorial aspirations concerning distribution, and that many such works never entered wide circulation. A famous contemporary example is the *Historia ecclesiastica* of Orderic Vitalis (1075–c.1152). Orderic's work was accessible in his own monastic library of St Evroult to those who had an interest, as is demonstrated by several known extracts from it. However, the only existing manuscript of the work as such is Orderic's own autograph.[194] To judge by the massive volume of his writing and its largely very local content, Orderic never seriously sought wider literary fame, his work being principally intended for himself and his family, that is, the present and future brethren of St Evroult. Gervase of Canterbury (b. *c.*1145, d. in or after 1210) formulated this sentiment, probably widely shared by monastic writers of historical texts, when he stated that his work was not intended for 'the public library' (*biblioteca publica*) but only for his own community.[195] The intention to contribute to the *biblioteca publica*, that is, to make one's work generally available in the public sphere, certainly set William, Henry, and Geoffrey apart from Orderic, Gervase, and many other monastic historians.

The second important observation that a comparative examination yields is that the social and cultural context in which the publishing took

---

[194] On extracts made of Orderic's history, M. Chibnall, *The Ecclesiastical History of Orderic Vitalis*, vol. 1 (Oxford: Clarendon Press, 1980), pp. 112–15.

[195] 'Me autem inter cronicae scriptores computandum non esse censeo, quia non bibliotecae publicae sed tibi, mi frater Thoma, et nostra familiolae pauperculae scribo'; Gervase of Canterbury, *Opera historica*, vol. 1, ed. W. Stubbs, Rolls Series, 73 (London: Longman, 1879), p. 89.

place – the publishing framework – had great significance in determining what authorial aspiration could hope to achieve. Between the late tenth and early twelfth centuries, many German writers, for instance, composed ambitious secular histories, comparable in style, substance, and, probably, their intended audience to the works of Henry, William, and Geoffrey. These engaging narratives, such as Widukind of Corvey's *Res gestae Saxonicae*, Thietmar of Merseburg's *Chronicon*, Wipo's *Gesta Chuonradi*, and the anonymous *Vita Heinrici IV*, have been much studied by modern scholars.[196] The manuscript record of their early circulation is, however, singularly unimpressive. Of *Res gestae Saxonicae* (967–73), there is one copy predating 1100, one from the twelfth century, and three later ones.[197] Thietmar of Merseburg's *Chronicon* (1018), a less polished work in literary terms, survives in one manuscript predating 1100 and in one other, later copy.[198] The anonymous *Vita Heinrici IV* similarly exists in one copy from the early twelfth century,[199] while the earliest manuscript of Wipo's *Gesta Chuonradi* (1040–6) dates only from the end of the sixteenth century.[200] While the German case is probably the most extreme one, a similar picture emerges if we look at the distribution of newly composed historical works in France and Normandy in the era preceding that of our three authors.

[196] For previous scholarship, see S. Bagge, *Kings, Politics and the Right Order of the World in German Historiography, c. 950–1150* (Leiden: Brill, 2002), *passim*.

[197] G. Waitz, K. A. Kehr, P. Hirsch, and H.-E. Lohmann, 'Einleitung', in *Rerum gestarum saxonicarum libri tres*. Monumenta Germaniae Historica. Scriptores rerum Germanicarum in usum scholarum separatim editi, 60 (Hannover: Hahn, 1935), pp. v–liii, at pp. xxx–xxxviii.

[198] R. Holtzmann, 'Einleitung', in *Thietmari Merseburgensis episcopi chronicon*. Monumenta Germaniae Historica. Scriptores rerum Germanicarum, Nova series 9 (Berlin: Weidmann, 1935), pp. vii–xlii, at pp. xxxiii–xxxix.

[199] W. Eberhard, 'Prefatio editoris', in *Vita Heinrici IV. Imperatoris*. Monumenta Germaniae Historica. Scriptores rerum Germanicarum in usum scholarum separatim editi, 58 (Hannover: Hahn, 1899), pp. 1–8, at p. 3.

[200] H. Bresslau, 'Einleitung', in *Wiponis Opera*. Monumenta Germaniae Historica. Scriptores rerum Germanicarum in usum scholarum separatim editi, 61 (Hannover: Hahn, 1915), pp. vii–lix, at pp. lix–l.

Rodulf Glaber's (*c*.980–*c*.1046) *Historiarum libri quinque* survives in one eleventh-century manuscript, which is in part autograph.[201] Aimoin of Fleury's *Historia Francorum* (*c*.998) exists in five copies, of which one is dated to the turn of the tenth century, one to the twelfth, and the remainder to later times.[202] Adémar of Chabannes's (989–1034) *Chronicon* has a slightly more impressive record of thirteen manuscripts, with three from the eleventh century and six from the twelfth.[203] In Normandy, the fact that there is one surviving medieval manuscript of *Carmen de Hastingae praelio*,[204] and none at all of *Gesta Guillelmi*, suggests strikingly limited circulation for those histories occasioned by the Norman Conquest.[205]

At the turn of the eleventh century, the circulation of historical texts appears, however, to have gained momentum. This can be seen in the intensified circulation of earlier works, such as Dudo of Saint-Quentin's *Historia Normannorum* (996–1015), which survives in only two eleventh-century manuscripts but in ten from the twelfth century or the beginning

[201] Paris, Bibliothèque nationale de France, MS lat. 10912. The other manuscripts are from the fifteenth and sixteenth centuries. See M. Frassetto, 'Rodulf Glaber', in G. Dunphy and C. Bratu (eds.), *Encyclopedia of the Medieval Chronicle* (Leiden: Brill, 2010), http://dx.doi.org.libproxy.helsinki.fi/10.1163/2213–2139_emc_SIM_02207, accessed 4 December 2017.

[202] G. H. Pertz (eds.), *Archiv der Gesellschaft für ältere deutsche Geschichtskunde*, vol. 7 (Hannover: Hahnicshen Hofbuchhandlung, 1839), pp. 554–6. Since this list leaves some ambiguities about the dates (and indeed shelfmarks) of the manuscripts, I give here my interpretation of it: Copenhagen, Det Kongelige Bibliotek, MS GKS 599 2:o (s. x/xi); London, British Library, MS Harley 3974 (s. xii); Oxford, Bodleian Library, MS Bodley 755 (s. xiii); Paris, Bibliothèque nationale de France, MS lat. 5925 (s. xiv) and MS lat. 5925A (s. xv).

[203] P. Bourgain, R. Landes, and G. Pon, *Ademari Cabannensis opera omnia. Pars 1, Chronicon*. Corpus Christianorum. Continuatio medievalis 129 (Turnhout: Brepols, 1999), pp. xiii–xxiv.

[204] C. Morton and H. Muntz, 'Introduction', in *The Carmen de Hastingae proelio of Guy of Amiens* (Oxford: Clarendon Press, 1972), pp. xv–lxxiv, at p. lix.

[205] R. Foreville, 'Introduction', in *Guillaume de Poitiers, Histoire de Guillaume le Conquérant* (Paris: Les Belles Lettres, 1952), vii–lxvi, at pp. l–liii.

of the thirteenth.[206] Dudo's continuation, William of Jumièges's *Gesta Normannorum Ducum* (*c.*1050–66), similarly exists in one eleventh-century but twenty twelfth-century copies.[207] Even more notably, the numbers of manuscripts of the newly published crusading histories of Guibert of Nogent (*Gesta Dei per Francos*, *c.*1112, thirty-four twelfth-century copies),[208] Baldric of Bourgueil (*Historia Hierosolimitana*, *c.*1107–8, at least eleven twelfth-century copies),[209] and Robert the Monk (*Historia Iherosolimitana*, after 1107, seven twelfth-century copies)[210] indicates that they found an audience more quickly and more effectively than had been the case for historical writing in the previous era. While the reliability of the numbers of manuscripts as indicators of popularity can of course be challenged, the oddities of survival should not in this case distort the overall picture, as it is highly unlikely that the survival rate of eleventh-century historical manuscripts would have been drastically worse than that of manuscripts of the same genre from the twelfth century.[211]

---

[206] For the manuscripts, see B. Pohl, *Dudo of Saint-Quentin's* Historia Normannorum: *Tradition, Innovation and Memory* (York: York Medieval Press, 2015), pp. 34–108.

[207] E. M. C. van Houts, *Gesta Normannorum Ducum: Een Studie Over De Handschriften, De Tekst, Het Geschiedwerk En Het Genre* (Groningen: [E. M. C. van Houts], 1982).

[208] C. Sweetenham, 'Guibert de Nogent', in G. Dunphy and C. Bratu (eds.), *Encyclopedia of the Medieval Chronicle* (Leiden: Brill, 2010), http://dx.doi.org.libproxy.helsinki.fi/10.1163/2213-2139_emc_SIM_01200, accessed 9 December 2017.

[209] S. Biddlecombe, 'Introduction', in *The Historia Ierosolimitana of Baldric of Bourgueil* (Woodbridge: Boydell Press, 2014), pp. ix–cvii, at pp. lxxvii–ci, dates eight manuscripts to the twelfth century and thirteen to the thirteenth century. However, these datings are mostly from catalogues, some of which are very old. Three manuscripts dated to the thirteenth century which I have examined seem rather to date from the twelfth century: Città del Vaticano, BAV, MS Reg. lat. 631; London, BL, MS Stowe 56, and Paris, BnF, MS lat. 5135.

[210] M. G. Bull and D. Kempf, 'Introduction', in *The* Historia Iherosolimitana *of Robert the Monk* (Woodbridge: Boydell & Brewer, 2013), pp. ix–lxxiv, at pp. lxv–lxxiv.

[211] See the discussion in J. Tahkokallio, 'The Classicization of the Latin Curriculum and the "Renaissance of the Twelfth Century": A Quantitative Study of the

This admittedly superficial examination of the levels of success of various historical works suggests that, around the year 1100, the patterns of textual transmission and book production were going through a transition. It is not difficult to connect this change with well-known developments in society: rapid economic growth, increasing demand for specialists in the written word, and an explosion in the availability of education, captured by Guibert of Nogent's famous remark as to how it had been next to impossible to find a decent grammarian in his youth (1060s), whereas wandering clerks skilled in Latin were now (*c.*1115) widely available.[212] I propose that it was this development of the infrastructure of written culture, the publishing framework, that opened the door for effective authorial publishing.

The method that William, Henry, and Geoffrey used to distribute their texts in this increasingly dynamic literary environment was to involve several people, who held nodal positions in this framework, in the process of publishing – that is, to construct a publishing circle. By way of conclusion, it will be appropriate to recapitulate the key elements of these circles: their personnel and the role these persons had in advancing textual distribution.

Many of the key contacts were forged at the presentation of the work or immediately thereafter and among them the dedicatees form a distinct group. The evidence of their impact on the texts' distribution is strong, even if rarely completely unambiguous. Some of the patrons we have encountered certainly loaned exemplars for others to read and copy and they must also have provided advertisement by word of mouth. Very probably they also commissioned new copies and participated in presenting copies to other notables. This is not to say that all patrons always did participate in the

Codicological Evidence', *Viator*, 46 (2016), 129–53, at 150–1 and 'Manuscripts as Evidence for the use of Classics in Education, c. 800–1200: Estimating the Randomness of Survival', *Interfaces*, 3 (2016), 28–45.

[212] Guibert de Nogent, *Histoire de sa vie*, ed. G. Bourgin (Paris: Librairie Alphonse Picard et fils, 1907), pp. 12–13: 'Erat paulo ante id temporis, et adhuc partim sub meo tempore tanta grammaticorum caritas, ut in oppidis prope nullus, in urbibus vix aliquis reperiri potuisset, et quos inveniri contigerat, eorum scientia tenuis erat, nec etiam moderni temporis clericulis vagantibus comparari poterat.'

distribution. Empress Matilda does not seem to have advanced the circulation of the *GRA*; and, while Alexander of Lincoln quite possibly made the *HA* available at Le Bec, his role as a literary patron remains ambiguous. Moreover, as Geoffrey's criticism of Alexander suggests, securing help in the distribution was not necessarily the chief aim of a dedication, as the authors also had other sorts of gains, such as career advancement, on their minds. Nevertheless, an interested patron could give a great boost to dissemination and it would appear natural to suppose that such a boost was one thing – if rarely the only thing – that authors wished for as they constructed the dedication to a literary work. Dedicatees were a very common, one might say near-integral, element of a successful publishing circle in this twelfth-century context.

However, especially when it came to making exemplars available, other kinds of collaborators, such as monastic librarians, were also important partners. Since so little narrative or documentary evidence discusses the day-to-day business of circulating texts, most of these medieval publishing agents will remain unknown to us by name. In our evidence, the one such person, encountered in several roles, is Robert of Torigni. It appears probable that he and the book collections he managed provided the main continental distribution platform for the early circulation of both *DGB* and the *HA*. For William of Malmesbury, the libraries of Glastonbury Abbey and Winchester Cathedral seem to have functioned in somewhat similar fashion. Success in getting a good exemplar into an active institutional library was paramount for the circulation of the works of the authors discussed here, just as it was for those authors whose own institutions provided the textual base. It is often difficult to say whether, and to what degree, the institutional librarians (or bibliophiles, if 'librarian' is too problematic a word) were intentionally recruited by the author and, as a consequence, how integral their role can be understood to have been to the authorial publishing circle. Nevertheless, authors must have been aware of the significance of institutional librarians and, given that they were seeking distribution, it would be very surprising if they had not taken measures to try to attain presence and visibility in the book collections of, say, Le Bec, or Glastonbury, to which they knew interested people would come for texts.

Finally, while this study has been about writers who can, in their twelfth-century context, be described as literary, it should be borne in mind that the actual constituents of a publishing circle would have been similar for most sorts of authors, whether or not they were members of religious institutions or whether or not they presented their works to dedicatees. The study of publishing in the manuscript context is still a new field and I propose that one of its main objectives should be the reconstruction of such publishing circles for individual works or groups of works.[213] At the same time, the publishing circles discussed in this Element call for due caution to be exercised in seeking to categorise the publication of texts in manuscript context by (more or less) fixed typologies, such as publishing by patronage, publishing 'officially', or publishing 'organically'. Such categorisations, when they are not closely based on empirical studies, risk imposing artificial interpretative categories on historical reality. They also have the tendency to obscure human agency, on which all these forms of textual circulation depended. Official sanction of a text by a religious order, or the author's membership of a religious house with strong networks and its own lettered tradition, may have helped in creating an effective publishing circle. But the circle was always made up of a particular constellation of individuals. It was these individuals on whom a work's entry into the contemporary literary canon depended.

---

[213] A database of medieval publishing networks, to facilitate this kind of inspection, is currently being produced under the auspices of the MedPub project and the Helsinki University, led by Prof. Samu Niskanen (samu.niskanen@helsinki.fi).

References

Manuscripts Cited

Aberystwyth, National Library of Wales, MS 11611

Aberystwyth, National Library of Wales, MS Peniarth 42

Aberystwyth, National Library of Wales, MS Peniarth 382

Aberystwyth, National Library of Wales, MS Porkington 17

Auxerre, Bibliothèque municipale, MS 91

Avranches, Bibliothèque municipale, MS 159

Baltimore, Walters Art Gallery, MS W 793

Berlin, Staatsbibliothek, MS theol. lat. qu. 328

Bern, Burgerbibliothek, MS 568

Brussels, Bibliothèque royale, MS 9871–9874

Cambridge, Corpus Christi College, MS 43

Cambridge, Corpus Christi College, MS 92

Cambridge, Corpus Christi College, MS 280

Cambridge, Corpus Christi College, MS 281

Cambridge, Corpus Christi College, MS 373

Cambridge, Gonville & Caius College, MS 103/55

Cambridge, Gonville & Caius College, MS 406/627

Cambridge, Trinity College, MS O. 2. 21

Cambridge, Trinity College, MS R. 5. 40

Cambridge, Trinity College, MS R. 7. 10

Cambridge, Trinity College, collection of Prof. S. D. Keynes

Cambridge, University Library, MS Dd. 6. 7

Cambridge, University Library, MS Dd. 6. 12

Cambridge, University Library, MS Ff. 1. 25

Cambridge, University Library, MS Gg. 2. 21

Cambridge, University Library, MS Ii. 1. 14

Cambridge, University Library, MS Ii. 2. 3

Cambridge, University Library, MS Ii 4. 4

Cambridge, University Library, MS Mm. 1. 34.

Città del Vaticano, Biblioteca Apostolica Vaticana, MS Reg. lat. 692

Città del Vaticano, Biblioteca Apostolica Vaticana, MS Reg. lat. 807

Città del Vaticano, Biblioteca Apostolica Vaticana, MS Vat. lat. 2005

Copenhagen, Det Kongelige Bibliotek, MS GKS 599 2:o

Douai, Bibliothèque municipale, MS 880

Douai, Bibliothèque municipale, MS 882

Durham, Ushaw College, MS 6

Edinburgh, National Library of Scotland, MS Advocates' 33.5.2.

Edinburgh, National Library of Scotland, MS Advocates' 33.5.4

Glasgow, University Library, MS Hunter U.6.6

Leiden, Universiteitsbibliotheek, MS BPL 20

Liège, Bibliothèques de l'Université de Liège, MS 369C

Lincoln, Cathedral Library, MS 214

London, British Library, MS Additional 23147

London, British Library, MS Additional 24061

London, British Library, MS Additional 38129

London, British Library, MS Arundel 35

London, British Library, MS Arundel 48

London, British Library, MS Arundel 161

London, British Library, MS Cotton Claudius A. V

London, British Library, MS Cotton Claudius C. IX

London, British Library, MS Cotton Titus A. XVIII

London, British Library, MS Cotton Vespasian B. X

London, British Library, Cotton Fragments XXIX

London, British Library, MS Egerton 3668

London, British Library, Harley 2

London, British Library, MS Harley 225

London, British Library, MS Harley 261
London, British Library, MS Harley 3641
London, British Library, MS Harley 3974
London, British Library, MS Lansdowne 732
London, British Library, MS Royal 13 B. XIX
London, British Library, MS Royal 13 D. II
London, British Library, MS Royal 13 D. V
London, Lambeth Palace, MS 179
London, Lambeth Palace Library, MS 188
London, Lambeth Palace Library, MS 327
London, Lambeth Palace Library, MS 454
Madrid, Biblioteca Nacional de España, MS 6319
Montpellier, Bibliothèque interuniversitaire, MS 92
New Haven (CT), Yale University Library, MS 590
Oxford, All Souls College, MS 33
Oxford, All Souls College, MS 35
Oxford, All Souls College, MS b. 32, no. 22
Oxford, Bodleian Library, MS Add. A.61
Oxford, Bodleian Library, MS Bodley 357
Oxford, Bodleian Library, MS Bodley 514
Oxford, Bodleian Library, MS Bodley 585
Oxford, Bodleian Library, MS Bodley 755
Oxford, Bodleian Library, MS Bodley 956
Oxford, Bodleian Library, MS Fairfax 28
Oxford, Bodleian Library, MS Hatton 54
Oxford, Bodleian Library, MS Jones 48
Oxford, Bodleian Library, MS Laud Misc. 548
Oxford, Bodleian Library, MS Laud Misc. 564
Oxford, Bodleian Library, MS Laud Misc. 598
Oxford, Bodleian Library, MS Laud Misc. 720

Oxford, Bodleian Library, MS Rawlinson B. 148

Oxford, Bodleian Library, MS Rawlinson B. 199

Oxford, Bodleian Library, MS Rawlinson C. 152

Oxford, Lincoln College, MS lat. 27

Oxford, Magdalen College, MS lat. 172

Paris, Bibliothèque nationale de France, MS lat. 2935

Paris, Bibliothèque nationale de France, MS lat. 5233

Paris, Bibliothèque nationale de France, MS lat. 5925

Paris, Bibliothèque nationale de France, MS lat. 5925A

Paris, Bibliothèque nationale de France, MS lat. 6040

Paris, Bibliothèque nationale de France, MS lat. 6041B

Paris, Bibliothèque nationale de France, MS lat. 6042

Paris, Bibliothèque nationale de France, MS lat. 6047

Paris, Bibliothèque nationale de France, MS lat. 6048

Paris, Bibliothèque nationale de France, MS lat. 6231

Paris, Bibliothèque nationale de France, MS lat. 6237

Paris, Bibliothèque nationale de France, MS lat. 6274

Paris, Bibliothèque nationale de France, MS lat. 8501A

Paris, Bibliothèque nationale de France, MS lat. 10185

Paris, Bibliothèque nationale de France, MS lat. 12943

Paris, Bibliothèque nationale de France, MS lat. 15172

Paris, Bibliothèque nationale de France, MS lat. 17569

Paris, Bibliothèque nationale de France, MS lat. 18271

Paris, Bibliothèque Sainte-Geneviève, MS 2113

Philadelphia, Free Library, MS Lewis E. 247

Princeton, University Library, MS Scheide 159

Rouen, Bibliothèque municipale, MS U.74

Rouen, Bibliothèque municipale, MS U.102

Rouen, Bibliothèque municipale, MS Y.15

Salisbury, Cathedral Library, MS 121

Stonyhurst, Stonyhurst College, MS 26

Troyes, Médiathèque du Grand Troyes, MS 6

Troyes, Médiathèque du Grand Troyes, MS 177

Troyes, Médiathèque du Grand Troyes, MS 273bis

Troyes, Médiathèque du Grand Troyes, MS 294bis

Printed Primary Sources

Alfred of Beverley, *Annales*, ed. T. Hearne (Oxford: E Theatro Sheldoniano, 1716).

Cronne, H. A., H. W. C. Davis, and R. H. C. Davis (eds.), *Regesta Regum Anglo-Normannorum 1066–1154, vol. 3, Regesta Regis Stephani ac Mathildis Imperatricis ac Gaufridi et Henrici Ducum Normannorum 1135–1154* (Oxford: Clarendon Press, 1968).

Geffrei Gaimar, *Estoire des Engleis*, ed. I. Short (Oxford: Oxford University Press, 2009).

Geoffrey of Monmouth, *De gestis Britonum*, ed. M. Reeve, trans. N. Wright (Woodbridge: Boydell & Brewer, 2007).

    Life of Merlin: Vita Merlini, ed. B. Clarke (Cardiff: University of Wales Press, 1973).

Gervase of Canterbury, *Opera historica*, vol. 1, ed. W. Stubbs, Rolls Series, 73 (London: Longman, 1879).

Guibert de Nogent, *Histoire de sa vie*, ed. G. Bourgin (Paris: Librairie Alphonse Picard et fils, 1907).

Henry of Huntingdon, *Anglicanus ortus: A Verse Herbal of the Twelfth Century*, ed. by W. Black (Toronto: Pontifical Institute of Mediaeval Studies, 2012)

    Historia Anglorum, ed. and trans. D. Greenway (Oxford: Clarendon Press, 1996).

Johnson, C., and H. A. Cronne (eds.), *Regesta Regum Anglo-Normannorum 1066–1154, vol. 2, Regesta Henrici Primi 1100–1135* (Oxford: Clarendon Press, 1956).

Orderic Vitalis, *Historia ecclesiastica*, ed. and trans. M. Chibnall, 6 vols. (Oxford: Clarendon Press, 1969–80).

William of Malmesbury, *Gesta Regum Anglorum: The History of the English Kings*, ed. R. M. Thomson and M. Winterbottom, 2 vols. (Oxford: Clarendon Press, 1998–9).

   Historia Novella, ed. E. King, trans. K. R. Potter (Oxford: Clarendon Press, 1998).

Secondary Works

Arnold, T., 'Introduction', in *Henrici Archidiaconi Huntendunensis Historia Anglorum*, Rolls Series 74, ed. T. Arnold (London: Longman & Co., 1879), pp. i–lxvi.

Ashe, L., *Fiction and History in England, 1066–1200* (Cambridge: Cambridge University Press, 2008).

Aurell, M., *Le Chevalier lettré: Savoir et conduite de l'aristocratie aux XIIe et XIIIe siécles* ([Paris]: Fayard, 2011).

   La Légende Du Roi Arthur: 550–1250 (Paris: Perrin, 2007).

Avril, F., 'A quand remontent les premiers ateliers d'enlumineurs laïcs à Paris', *Les Dossiers de l'archéologie*, 16 (1976), 36–44.

Bagge, S., *Kings, Politics and the Right Order of the World in German Historiography, c. 950–1150* (Leiden: Brill, 2002).

Bennett, H. S., 'The Production and Dissemination of Vernacular Manuscripts in the Fifteenth Century', *The Library*, Fifth Series, 1 (1946–7), 167–78.

Berg, K., *Studies in Tuscan Twelfth-Century Illumination* (Oslo: Universitetsforlaget, 1968).

Biddlecombe, S., 'Introduction', in *The Historia Ierosolimitana of Baldric of Bourgueil* (Woodbridge: Boydell Press, 2014), pp. ic–cvii.

Bishop, T. A. M., 'Notes on Cambridge Manuscripts', *Transactions of the Cambridge Bibliographical Society*, 2 (1954–8), 185–99.

Black, W., 'Henry of Huntingdon's Lapidary Rediscovered and His Anglicanus Ortus Reassembled', *Mediaeval Studies*, 68 (2006), 43–88.

Bourgain, P., R. Landes, and G. Pon, *Ademari Cabannensis opera omnia. Pars 1, Chronicon*. Corpus Christianorum. Continuatio medievalis, 129 (Turnhout: Brepols, 1999).

Bresslau, H., 'Einleitung', *Wiponis Opera*. Monumenta Germaniae Historica. Scriptores rerum Germanicarum in usum scholarum separatim editi, 61 (Hannover: Hahn, 1915), pp. vii–lix.

Brugger, E., 'Zu Galfrid von Monmouth's *Historia Regum Britanniae*', *Zeitschrift für französische Sprache und Literatur*, 57 (1933), 257–312.

Bull, M. G., and D. Kempf, 'Introduction', in *The* Historia Iherosolimitana *of Robert the Monk* (Woodbridge: Boydell & Brewer, 2013), pp. ix–lxxiv.

Burton, J. E., *The Monastic Order in Yorkshire, 1069–1215* (Cambridge: Cambridge University Press, 1999).

Campbell, J., 'Some Twelfth-Century Views of the Anglo-Saxon Past', in J. Campbell, *Essays in Anglo-Saxon History* (London: The Hambledon Press, 1986), pp. 209–28.

Catalogue général des manuscrits des bibliothèques publiques de France. Départements. Série in-quarto, 2 (Paris: Bibliothèque nationale de France, 1855).

Chibnall, M., *The Empress Matilda: Queen Consort, Queen Mother, and Lady of the English* (Oxford: Blackwell, 1991).

   The Ecclesiastical History of Orderic Vitalis, vol. 1 (Oxford: Clarendon Press, 1980).

   'Introduction', in Orderic Vitalis, *Historia ecclesiastica*, vol. 6, ed. and trans. M. Chibnall (Oxford: Clarendon Press, 1978), pp. xvii–xxvii.

Christianson, C. P., 'The Rise of London's Book-Trade', in L. Hellinga and J. B. Trapp (eds.), *The Cambridge History of the Book in Britain*, vol. 3 (Cambridge: Cambridge University Press, 1999), pp. 128–47.

Clanchy, M. T., *From Memory to Written Record: England 1066–1307*, 2nd ed. (Oxford: Blackwell, 1993).

Cooper, A., '"The Feet of Those That Bark Shall Be Cut off": Timorous Historians and the Personality of Henry I', *Anglo-Norman Studies*, 23 (2000), 47–67.

Crick, J., Historia Regum Britannie *of Geoffrey of Monmouth III: A Summary Catalogue of the Manuscripts* (Cambridge: D.S.Brewer, 1989).

   Historia Regum Britannie *of Geoffrey of Monmouth IV: Dissemination and Reception in the Later Middle Ages* (Cambridge: D.S.Brewer, 1991).

   'Two Newly Located Manuscripts of Geoffrey of Monmouth's *Historia regum Britanniae*', *Arthurian Literature*, 13 (1995), 151–6.

Crick, J., and A. Walsham, 'Introduction: Script, Print and History', in J. Crick and A. Walsham (eds.), *The Uses of Script and Print, 1300–1700* (Cambridge: Cambridge University Press, 2004), pp. 1–26.

Crouch, D., *The Reign of King Stephen, 1135–1154* (Harlow: Longman, 2000).

   'Robert, Earl of Gloucester, and the Daughter of Zelophehad', *Journal of Medieval History*, 11 (1985), 227–43.

Dalton, P., 'The Date of Geoffrey Gaimar's *Estoire des Engleis*, the Connections of his Patrons, and the Politics of Stephen's Reign', *The Chaucer Review*, 42 (2007), 23–47.

Delhaye, P., 'L'Organisation scolaire au XIIe siècle', *Traditio*, 5 (1947), 211–68.

Delisle, L., 'Introduction', in *Chronique de Robert de Torigni*, vol. 1 (Rouen: A. Le Brument, 1872), pp. i–lxxi.

Dempster, G., 'Manly's Conception of the Early History of the Canterbury Tales', *PMLA*, 61 (1946), 379–415.

Doyle, A. I., 'Publication by Members of the Religious Orders', in J. Griffiths and D. Pearsall (eds.), *Book Production and Publishing in Britain 1375–1475* (Cambridge: Cambridge University Press, 1989), pp. 109–23.

Dumville, D. N., 'An Early Text of Geoffrey of Monmouth's *Historia Regum Britanniae* and the Circulation of Some Latin Histories in Twelfth-Century Normandy', *Arthurian Literature*, 4 (1985), 1–36.

Dunning, A. N. J, 'Alexander Neckam's Manuscripts and the Augustinian Canons of Oxford and Cirencester', unpublished PhD dissertation, University of Toronto (2016).

Earp, L., 'Machaut's Role in the Production of Manuscripts of His Works', *Journal of the American Musicological Society*, 42 (1989), 461–503.

Eberhard, W., 'Prefatio editoris', in *Vita Heinrici IV. Imperatoris*. Monumenta Germaniae Historica. Scriptores rerum Germanicarum in usum scholarum separatim editi, 58 (Hannover: Hahn, 1899), pp. 1–8.

Eckhardt, C., 'Geoffrey of Monmouth's *Prophetia Merlini* and the construction of Liège University MS 369C', *Manuscripta*, 32 (1988), 176–84.

Eisenstein, E. L., *The Printing Press as an Agent of Change: Communications and Cultural Transformations in Early Modern Europe*, vol. 1 (Cambridge: Cambridge University Press, 1979).

Evergates, T., *The Aristocracy in the County of Champagne, 1100–1300* (Philadelphia: University of Pennsylvania Press, 2007).

Farmer, D. H., 'William of Malmesbury's Life and Works', *The Journal of Ecclesiastical History*, 13 (1962), 39–54.

Fasti Ecclesiae Anglicanae 1066–1300, vol. 3, Lincoln (London: Institute of Historical Research, 1977).

Fletcher, R. H., *The Arthurian Material in the Chronicles, Especially Those of Great Britain and France* (Cambridge, MA: Harvard University Press, 1906).

Foreville, R., 'L'École de Caen au XIe siècle et les origines normandes de l'université d'Oxford', in *Études médiévales offertes à M. Le Doyen Augustin Fliche de l'Institut* (Montpellier: Ch. Déhan, 1952), pp. 81–100.

'Introduction', in *Guillaume de Poitiers, Histoire de Guillaume le Conquérant* (Paris: Les Belles Lettres, 1952), pp. vii–lxvi.

Frassetto, M., 'Rodulf Glaber', in G. Dunphy and C. Bratu (eds.), *Encyclopedia of the Medieval Chronicle* (Leiden: Brill, 2010), http://dx.doi.org.libproxy.helsinki.fi/10.1163/2213–2139_emc_SIM_02207, accessed 4 December 2017.

Gillingham, J., 'The Beginnings of English Imperialism', *Journal of Historical Sociology*, 5 (1992), 392–409.

'The Context and Purposes of Geoffrey of Monmouth's History of the Kings of Britain', in J. Gillingham, *English in the Twelfth Century* (Woodbridge: Boydell Press, 2000), pp. 19–39.

'Henry of Huntingdon and the Twelfth-Century Revival of the English Nation', in J. Gillingham, *English in the Twelfth Century* (Woodbridge: Boydell Press, 2000), pp. 123–44.

'Henry of Huntingdon in His Time (1135) and Place (between Lincoln and the Royal Court)', in K. Stopka (ed.), *Gallus Anonymous and His Chronicle in the Context of Twelfth-Century Historiography from the Perspective of the Latest Research* (Cracow: Polish Academy of Arts and Sciences, 2010), pp. 157–72.

Giraud, C., *Per verba magistri: Anselme de Laon et son école au XIIe siècle*. Bibliothèque d'histoire culturelle du Moyen Âge (Turnhout: Brepols, 2010).

Gransden, A., *Historical Writing in England: c. 550 to c. 1307* (Ithaca, NY: Cornell University Press, 1974).

Greenway, D. 'Henry [Henry of Huntingdon] (c. 1088–c. 1157), Historian and Poet', in Oxford Dictionary of National Biography, https://doi-org.libproxy.helsinki.fi/10.1093/ref:odnb/12970, accessed 4 April 2018.

'Henry of Huntingdon and the Manuscripts of His *Historia Anglorum*', *Anglo-Norman Studies*, 11 (1987), 103–26.

'Henry of Huntingdon as Poet: The *De Herbis* Rediscovered', *Medium Aevum*, 74 (2005), 329–32.

'Introduction', in Henry of Huntingdon, *Historia Anglorum*, ed. and trans. D. Greenway (Oxford: Clarendon Press, 1996), pp. xxiii–clxxii.

Griscom, A., 'The Date of Composition of Geoffrey of Monmouth's *Historia*: New Manuscript Evidence', *Speculum*, 1 (1926), 129–56.

The Historia Regum Britanniae *of Geoffrey of Monmouth* (London: Longmans, Green, 1929).

Gullick, M., 'Professional Scribes in Eleventh- and Twelfth-Century England', *English Manuscript Studies, 1100–1700*, 7 (1998), 1–24.

Hobbins, D., *Authorship and Publicity before Print: Jean Gerson and the Transformation of Late Medieval Learning* (Philadelphia: University of Pennsylvania Press, 2009).

Hollister, C. W., *Henry I* (New Haven, CT: Yale University Press, 2001).

Holzknecht, K. J., 'Literary Patronage in the Middle Ages', unpublished PhD dissertation, University of Pennsylvania (1923).

Holtzmann, R., 'Einleitung', in *Thietmari Merseburgensis episcopi chronicon*. Monumenta Germaniae Historica. Scriptores rerum Germanicarum, Nova series 9 (Berlin: Weidmann, 1935), pp. vii–xlii.

Jaeger, C. S., *The Envy of Angels: Cathedral Schools and Social Ideals in Medieval Europe, 950–1200* (Philadelphia: University of Pennsylvania Press, 1994).

Keeler, L., *Geoffrey of Monmouth and the Late Latin Chroniclers 1300–1500* (Berkeley: University of California, 1946).

Kempshall, M., *Rhetoric and the Writing of History, 400–1500* (Manchester: Manchester University Press, 2011).

King, E., 'Introduction', in William of Malmesbury, *Historia novella*, ed. E. King (Oxford: Clarendon Press, 1998), pp. xvii–cix.

Knowles, D., *The Monastic Order in England: A History of Its Development from the Times of St Dunstan to the Fourth Lateran Council 940–1216*, 2nd ed. (Cambridge: Cambridge University Press, 1963).

Könsgen, E. 'Zwei unbekannte Briefe zu den *Gesta Regum Anglorum* des Wilhelm von Malmesbury', *Deutsches Archiv für Erforschung des Mittelalters*, 31 (1975), 204–14.

Laidlaw, J. C., 'Christine de Pizan – a Publisher's Progress', *Modern Language Review*, 82 (1987), 35–75.

Liebermann, F., 'Heinrich von Huntingdon', *Forschungen Zur Deutschen Geschichte*, 18 (1878), 265–95.

Loomis, L. H., 'The Auchinleck Manuscript and a Possible London Bookshop of 1330–1340', *PMLA*, 57 (1942), 595–627.

Lucas, P. J., *From Author to Audience: John Capgrave and Medieval Publication* (Dublin: University College Dublin Press, 1997).

Madan, F., H. H. E. Craster, and N. Denholm-Young, *A Summary Catalogue of Western Manuscripts in the Bodleian Library at Oxford*, vol. 2, part 2 (Oxford: Clarendon Press, 1937).

Meehan, B. 'Geoffrey of Monmouth, *Prophecies of Merlin*: New Manuscript Evidence', *Bulletin of the Board of Celtic Studies*, 28 (1978), 37–46.

Meyvaert, P. 'Medieval Notions of Publication: The "Unpublished" *Opus Caroli Regis Contra Synodum* and the Council of Frankfort (794)', *The Journal of Medieval Latin*, 12 (2002), 78–89.

Morton, C., and H. Muntz, 'Introduction', in *The Carmen de Hastingae proelio of Guy of Amiens* (Oxford: Clarendon Press, 1972), pp. xv–lxxiv.

Nichols, S. G., 'Introduction: Philology in a Manuscript Culture', *Speculum*, 65 (1990), 1–10.

Nordenfalk, C., *Codex Caesareus Upsaliensis* (Stockholm: Almqvist & Wiksell, 1971).

Oram, R., *David I: The King Who Made Scotland* (Stroud: Tempus, 2004).

Paré, G., A. Brunet, and P. Tremblay, *La Renaissance du XIIᵉ siècle: Les écoles et l'enseignement* (Paris: J. Vrin, 1933).

Parkes, M. B., *Their Hands Before Our Eyes: A Closer Look at Scribes. The Lyell Lectures Delivered in the University of Oxford 1999* (Aldershot: Ashgate, 2008).

Pertz, G. H. (ed.), *Archiv der Gesellschaft für ältere deutsche Geschichtskunde*, vol. 7 (Hannover: Hahnicshen Hofbuchhandlung, 1839).

Pohl, B. '"Abbas Qui et Scriptor?": The Handwriting of Robert of Torigni and His Scribal Activity as Abbot of Mont-Saint-Michel (1154–1186)', *Traditio*, 69 (2014), 45–86.

   Dudo of Saint-Quentin's Historia Normannorum*: Tradition, Innovation and Memory* (York: York Medieval Press, 2015)

   'When Did Robert of Torigni First Receive Henry of Huntingdon's *Historia Anglorum*, and Why Does It Matter?', *The Haskins Society Journal*, 26 (2015), 143–68.

Poupardin, R. (ed.), *Recueil des chartes de Saint-Germain-des-Prés*, vol. 1 (Paris: Champion, 1909).

Reeve, M. D., 'Introduction', in Geoffrey of Monmouth, *De gestis Britonum*, ed. M. Reeve, trans. N. Wright (Woodbridge: Boydell & Brewer, 2007), pp. vii–lxxvi.

   'The Transmission of the *Historia Regum Britanniae*', *The Journal of Medieval Latin*, 1 (1991), 73–117

Riddy, F., '"Publication" before Print: The Case of Julian of Norwhich', in J. Crick and A. Walsham (eds.), *The Uses of Script and Print, 1300–1700* (Cambridge: Cambridge University Press, 2004), pp. 29–49.

Rigg, A. G., 'Henry of Huntingdon's Herbal', *Mediaeval Studies*, 65 (2003), 213–92.

Root, R. K., 'Publication before Printing', *PMLA*, 28 (1913), 417–31.

Rouse, R. H., and M. A. Rouse, 'Wandering Scribes and Travelling Artists: Raulinus of Fremington and His Bolognese Bible', in J. Brown and W. P. Stoneman (eds.), *A Distinct Voice. Medieval Studies in Honor of*

Leonard E. Boyle, O.P (Notre Dame, IN: University of Notre Dame Press, 1997), pp. 32–67.

Sharpe, R., 'Anselm as Author: Publishing in the Late Eleventh Century', *The Journal of Medieval Latin*, 19 (2009), 1–87.

English Benedictine Libraries: The Shorter Catalogues. Corpus of British Medieval Library Catalogues, vol. 4 (London: British Library, 1996).

Sheppard, J. M., *The Buildwas Books: Book Production, Acquisition and Use at an English Cistercian Monastery, 1165–c.1400* (Oxford: The Oxford Bibliographical Society, 1996).

Shonk, T. A., 'A Study of the Auchinleck Manuscript: Bookmen and Bookmaking in the Early Fourteenth Century', *Speculum*, 60 (1985), 71–91.

Short, I., 'Gaimar's Epilogue and Geoffrey of Monmouth's Liber Vetustissimus', *Speculum*, 69 (1994), 323–43.

Southern, R. W., 'Presidential Address: Aspects of the European Tradition of Historical Writing: 4. The Sense of the Past', *Transactions of the Royal Historical Society*, 23 (1973), 243–63.

Stacy, N. E., 'Henry of Blois and the Lordship of Glastonbury', *The English Historical Review*, 114 (1999), 1–33.

Stirnemann, P., 'Fils de la vierge: L'initiale à filigranes parisiennes: 1140–1314', *Revue de l'Art*, 90 (1990), 58–73.

'Où ont été fabriqués les livres de la glose ordinaire dans la première moitié du XIIe siècle?', in F. Gasparri (ed.), *Le XIIe siècle: Mutations et renouveau en France dans la première moitié du XIIe siècle* (Paris: Cahiers du Léopard d'Or, 1994), pp. 257–301.

'Two Twelfth-Century Bibliophiles and Henry of Huntingdon's *Historia Anglorum*', *Viator*, 24 (1993), 121–42.

Stubbs, W., 'Preface', in *Willelmi Malmesbiriensis monachi de gestis regum Anglorum libri quinque*, Rolls Series, 90, ed. W. Stubbs (London: Her

Majesty's Stationery Office by Eyre and Spottiswoode, 1887), pp. ix–cxlvii.

Sweetenham, C., 'Guibert de Nogent', in G. Dunphy and C. Bratu (eds.), *Encyclopedia of the Medieval Chronicle* (Leiden: Brill, 2010), http://dx.doi.org.libproxy.helsinki.fi/10.1163/2213-2139_emc_SIM_01200, accessed 9 December 2017.

Tahkokallio, J., 'The Classicization of the Latin Curriculum and the "Renaissance of the Twelfth Century": A Quantitative Study of the Codicological Evidence', *Viator*, 46 (2016), 129–53.

   'French Chroniclers and the Credibility of Geoffrey of Monmouth's *History of the Kings of Britain*, c. 1150–1225', in H. Tétrel and G. Veysseyre (eds.), *L'Historia regum Britannie et les 'Bruts en Europe': Traductions, adaptations, réappropriations (XIIe–XVIe siècle)* (Paris: Classiques Garnier, 2015), pp. 53–67.

   'Manuscripts as Evidence for the use of Classics in Education, c. 800–1200: Estimating the Randomness of Survival', *Interfaces*, 3 (2016), 28–45.

   'Update to the List of Manuscripts of Geoffrey of Monmouth's Historia regum Britanniae',*Arthurian Literature*, 32 (2015), 187–203.

Tatlock, J. S. P., *The Legendary History of Britain: Geoffrey of Monmouth's Historia Regum Britanniae and Its Early Vernacular Versions* (Berkley: University of California Press, 1950).

Tether, L., *Publishing the Grail in Medieval and Renaissance France* (Woodbridge: D.S.Brewer, 2017).

   'Revisiting the Manuscripts of Perceval and the Continuations: Publishing Practices and Authorial Transition', *Journal of the International Arthurian Society*, 2 (2014), 20–45.

Thomson, R. M., 'Introduction', in William of Malmesbury, *Gesta Pontificum Anglorum: The History of the English Bishops*, vol. 2, ed. R. M. Thomson and M. Winterbottom (Oxford: Clarendon Press, 2007), pp. xix–liii.

'Malmesbury, William of (b. c. 1090, d. in or after 1142), Historian, Man of Letters, and Benedictine Monk', *Oxford Dictionary of National Biography*, www.oxforddnb.com/view/10.1093/ref:odnb/9780198614128.001.0001 /odnb-9780198614128-e-29461, accessed 4 April 2018.

William of Malmesbury, rev. ed. (Woodbridge: Boydell Press, 2003).

Thomson, R. M., and M. Winterbottom, 'Introduction', in William of Malmesbury, *Gesta Regum Anglorum: The History of the English Kings*, vol. 1, ed. R. Thomson and M. Winterbottom (Oxford: Clarendon Press, 1998), pp. xiii–xxxii.

'Introduction', in William of Malmesbury, *Gesta Regum Anglorum: The History of the English Kings*, vol. 2, ed. R. Thomson and M. Winterbottom (Oxford: Clarendon Press, 1999), pp. xvii–xlvii.

Tolhurst, F., *Geoffrey of Monmouth and the Translation of Female Kingship* (Basingstoke: Palgrave Macmillan, 2013).

Trevitt, J., *Five Hundred Years of Printing by S.H. Steinberg*, rev. ed. (London: British Library and Oak Knoll Press, 1996).

van Houts, E. M. C., *Gesta Normannorum Ducum: Een Studie Over De Handschriften, De Tekst, Het Geschiedwerk En Het Genre* (Groningen: [E. M. C. van Houts], 1982).

Waitz, G., K. A. Kehr, P. Hirsch, and H.-E. Lohmann, 'Einleitung', *Rerum gestarum Saxonicarum libri tres*. Monumenta Germaniae Historica. Scriptores rerum Germanicarum in usum scholarum separatim editi, 60 (Hannover: Hahn, 1935), pp. v–liii.

Winkler, E. A., *Royal Responsibility in Anglo-Norman Historical Writing* (Oxford: Oxford University Press, 2017).

Winterbottom, M., 'Introduction', in William of Malmesbury, *Gesta Pontificum Anglorum. The History of the English Bishops*, vol. 1, ed. R. M. Thomson and M. Winterbottom (Oxford: Clarendon Press, 2007), pp. xi–xxxi.

Wright, N., 'Introduction', in *The* Historia regum Britannie *of Geoffrey of Monmouth, vol. 1: A Single-Manuscript Edition from Bern, Burgerbibliothek, Ms. 568*, ed. N. Wright (Cambridge: D.S.Brewer, 1985), pp. ix–lix.

  'The Place of Henry of Huntingdon's *Epistola ad Warinum* in the Text-History of Geoffrey of Monmouth's *Historia Regum Britannie*: A Preliminary Investigation', in G. Jondorf and D. N. Dumville (eds.), *France and the British Isles in the Middle Ages and Renaissance: Essays by Members of Girton College, Cambridge, in Memory of Ruth Morgan* (Woodbridge: Boydell Press, 1991), pp. 71–113.

Funding Information

This study has received funding from the European Union's Horizon 2020 research and innovation programme under grant agreement No 716538 (MedPub, Medieval Publishing from c. 1000 to 1500).

Cambridge Elements

Publishing and Book Culture

SERIES EDITOR
Samantha Rayner
University College London

Samantha Rayner is a Reader in UCL's Department of Information Studies. She is also Director of UCL's Centre for Publishing, co-Director of the Bloomsbury CHAPTER (Communication History, Authorship, Publishing, Textual Editing and Reading) and co-editor of the Academic Book of the Future BOOC (Book as Open Online Content) with UCL Press.

ASSOCIATE EDITOR
Rebecca Lyons
University of Bristol

Rebecca Lyons is a Teaching Fellow at the University of Bristol. She is also co-editor of the experimental BOOC (Book as Open Online Content) at UCL Press. She teaches and researches book and reading history, particularly female owners and readers of Arthurian literature in fifteenth- and sixteenth-century England, and also has research interests in digital academic publishing.

About the Series

This series aims to fill the demand for easily accessible, quality texts available for teaching and research in the diverse and dynamic fields of Publishing and Book Culture. Rigorously researched and peer-reviewed Elements will be published under themes, or 'Gatherings'. These Elements should be the first check point for researchers or students working on that area of publishing and book trade history and practice: we hope that, situated so logically at Cambridge University Press, where academic publishing in the UK began, it will develop to create an unrivalled space where these histories and practices can be investigated and preserved.

Cambridge Elements

Publishing and Book Culture Publishing the Canon

Gathering Editor: Leah Tether

Leah Tether is a Reader in Medieval Literature and Digital Cultures at the University of Bristol. Her research is on historical publishing practices from manuscript to digital, and she has a special interest in Arthurian literature of the Middle Ages. She is the author of Publishing the Grail in Medieval and Renaissance France (2017).

ELEMENTS IN THE GATHERING

Contingent Canons: African Literature and the Politics of Location
Madhu Krishnan
Publishing the Science Fiction Canon: The Case of Scientific Romance
Adam Roberts
The Anglo-Norman Historical Canon: Publishing and Manuscript Culture
Jaakko Tahkokallio

Publishing and Book Culture
the future